Sunrise Patrols

A Trooper's Story of Life in the British South African Police in the Late Nineteen-Twenties

John Edgar Palmer
Trooper (2829)

TSL Publications
The Great War in Africa Association

Published in Great Britain in 2021
By Great War in Africa Association, TSL Publications, Rickmansworth

ISBN: 978-1-913294-91-5

First published in 2008 by the United Kingdom Branch of the British South Africa Police Regimental Association. Second edition published 2010.

Copyright, unless otherwise stated, belongs to the United Kingdom Branch of the British South Africa Police Regimental Association.

All rights reserved. No part of this publication may be reproduced, stored in a retrieval system or transmitted in any form by any means; electronic, mechanical, photocopying, recording or otherwise, except brief extracts for the purpose of review, without written permission of the publisher and copyright owners.

Acknowledgement and thanks go to:

National Archives of Zimbabwe
The Outpost Magazine of the British South Africa Police
Cover Design: Alan Toms (7391)
Books of the BSAP Crest Design: Les Burrows (9591)
The History Section Committee, United Kingdom Branch Regimental Association
Alan Stock (6063), Editor of *The Outpost* 1966 to 1984

Arranged and typeset by John Berry

Apology is made for the standard of some photographs. This is caused by scanning from old magazines with poor paper quality.

CONTENTS

Chapter One	Depot	7
Chapter Two	To Bloemfontein	15
Chapter Three	Gwanda	19
Chapter Four	Relaxation	23
Chapter Five	My First Game Case Conviction	26
Chapter Six	To the Limpopo	28
Chapter Seven	My First Poacher	34
Chapter Eight	Nineteen Mile Stretch	38
Chapter Nine	Crocodiles	43
Chapter Ten	Limpopo Police Camp	46
Chapter Eleven	Mtetengwe	49
Chapter Twelve	Cowboys on the Rand	52
Chapter Thirteen	The Eland Hunters	56
Chapter Fourteen	Leopards and Lions	60
Chapter Fifteen	Extended Patrol	64
Chapter Sixteen	Sick Interlude	71
Chapter Seventeen	Fort Rixon	75
Chapter Eighteen	Motorbikes and Warlords	79
Chapter Nineteen	Exercise and Expertise	83
Chapter Twenty	Ostrich of Trouble	89
Chapter Twenty-One	Cock's Farm	94
Chapter Twenty-Two	From Business to Pleasure	102
Chapter Twenty-Three	Waterworks	111
Chapter Twenty-Four	Hunting Hilarity	116
Chapter Twenty-Five	Beitbridge	120
Chapter Twenty-Six	Language and Lip Service	125
Chapter Twenty-Seven	Sleuth-Hounds	129
Chapter Twenty-Eight	The Great Train Robberies	133
Chapter Twenty-Nine	Goodbye to Crime	142
Chapter Thirty	Spiritual Homecoming	144
Chapter Thirty-One	Back to Beitbridge	151
Chapter Thirty-Two	Of Snakes and Sealing Wax	155
Chapter Thirty-Three	More Border Trouble	160
Chapter Thirty-Four	Change of Scenery	165
Chapter Thirty-Five	Murder on the Gwaai	168
Chapter Thirty-Six	Last Act – Hamba Palma	181

Maps
Southern Rhodesia   page 6
Gwanda/Limpopo Areas   page 106

List of Photographs   pages 104/105
Trooper Palmer's Remount Squad
RSM 'Jock' Douglas
Mount Cazalet
Gwanda Police Camp
Outside Fort Rixon Police Station
Trooper Palmer with Mr Robinson and Corporal White
Trooper Palmer with Mail vehicle

Local map of locations of Trooper Palmer's Stories (page 106)
   Col. Edward's Inspection
   Preparing Dug-out canoes
   General Smuts
   Occupation of New Iringa
   'A' Service Company group
   Brig.-Gen. Northey
   Iringa Cemetery
   Archie Cripwell
   Motor Column photographs
   R.N.R. Recruits
   Rhodesia Native Regiment Officers
   R.N.R. photographs of F.G. Elliot
   R.N.R. in training

Facsimile of the heading to the first instalment of Sunrise Patrols, as published in the *OUTPOST* in February 1978, under the editorship of Alan Stock (6063). The series appeared over three years. Alan Stock also kindly provided the three dozen or so issues required to compile this book.

John Edgar Palmer joined the British South Africa Police as a Trooper in November 1926 and served until January 1933. He died in Serowe, Botswana, on 16 June 1978.

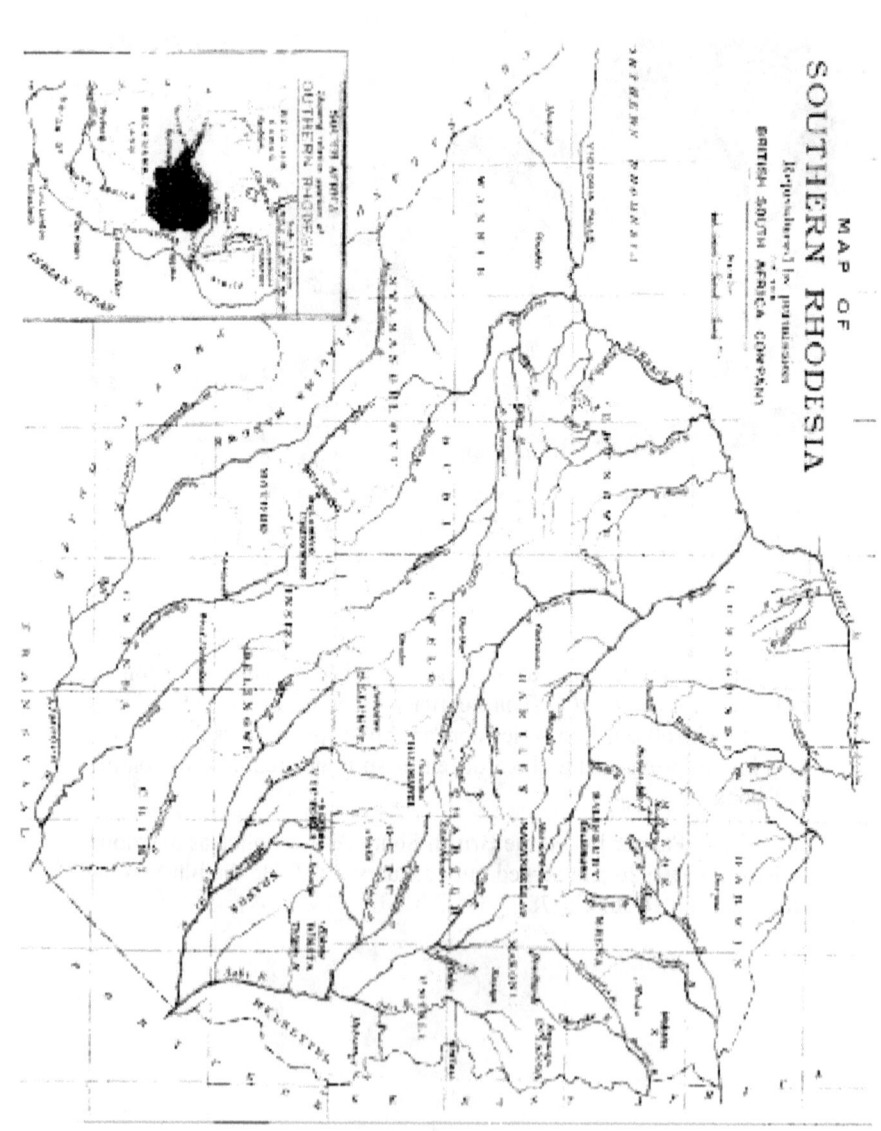

CHAPTER ONE

Depot

During the winter months of 1926 I was managing a trading station in Basutoland. There was snow on the Maluti Mountains and the Basutos were wise enough to remain in their grass-thatched huts so that business in the trading stores was inclined to be quiet. I remember I was rather depressed due, no doubt, to the cold weather. So when the mail came in with a letter from B.S.A. Police Headquarters in Salisbury I received quite a thrill. I had earlier made application to join this fine body of men but months had gone by with no word from Salisbury and I had begun to despair. The letter told me I had been accepted and gave instructions for me to proceed to Salisbury and report for attestation the following month.

Immediately I sat down and wrote to the owner of the trading store, tendering my resignation. He came out from Maseru the following weekend and we held a long discussion during which he tried to persuade me to change my mind. But I was adamant and eventually he arranged for stock to be taken so that I could get away as soon as possible.

Having handed over the keys to him I proceeded to Joel's Drift to say farewell to my parents. Dad then drove me to Fouriesburg where I caught the Kimberley-bound train. At Kimberley I caught the train from Capetown for Rhodesia.

On arrival at Bulawayo I was met by my cousin Mick who was already serving in the B.S.A. Police. He was in Bulawayo attending the High Court Session, to give evidence in a murder case. He was leaving that evening for Gwelo where he was due to take charge of the District Police. Consequently, I had good company as far as Gwelo, where I bid him farewell. In Salisbury the following morning I was met at the Station by the Depot buckwagon drawn by a couple of mules. Salisbury in those days was far different from the modern city it is today and I remember bumping over mud tracks with long grass growing right up to the road. In fact, I sat on the buckboard wondering at the wildness of the veld and expecting at every turn to see a lion or leopard cross the roadway! At the Depot the first man I saw was an old school pal and to make matters more pleasant for me, I was posted to his barrack room. He had joined up some three months before me and I was told that I was the eighth man to join the recruit squad of which he was a member. This meant that I had to borrow his notes on Musketry, Animal Management and Law and Police to catch up to other members of the squad. It meant night swotting for a couple of weeks and extra lessons on Law and Police to attain the standards of the others, a task which I eventually accomplished.

I caused a bit of a stir among my colleagues the first time I joined the squad for musketry practice. The instructor picked on me to give a demonstration of rapid fire. This meant that on the word "Go", I had to assume the prone position on the cement floor, load and "fire" ten rounds of dummy ammunition at a miniature target with a hole punctured through the centre of the black bull's-eye. The instructor meanwhile timed the minute allowed for the exercise and viewed the shottist's aim through the hole in the miniature target which he held to his eye. Each shot was declared – good, bad or indifferent. One had to count the rounds fired and reload from a bandolier the second clip of five dummy cartridges. Heaven help you if you did not count the rounds! Even the bandolier had to be refastened in the specified time. I had practised this exercise of an evening until my wrists became painful. In reloading, one was expected to roll the rifle to enable the smooth movement of the bolt in loading and unloading without disturbing the aim on the target. The instructor was watching all these points, at the same time marking off the seconds of the allowed minute. As I fired my last round I worked the bolt two or three times to show the magazine was clear, sprang to attention and came to the "Stand at ease" position. I was surprised to hear the instructor, a real critic where musketry was concerned, say "Very Good". At the end of the period, as we filed away, my half-section remarked, "What beats me is that a bloke who has just joined the squad could show up us older hands in 'rapid fire'." Little did he know that every evening I had sweated to practise this very exercise whilst he was enjoying himself at the Salisbury bioscopes.

Later in the course, when we reached the stage of actually firing on the Salisbury rifle range, I was the only member of our squad to reach the King's Medal Course of "Fire with

Movement." This entailed starting from the 500 yard mound firing two rounds, then to the 400 yard mound firing two more, then the 300 and the 200 yards with fixed bayonets, all in the prone position. Finally, with bayonets still fixed, one fired two rounds standing at the 100 yard mound and then went up into the butts to count the score and see how many "bulls" had been recorded. I was never presented with the King's Medal so my score must have been below standard. However, I did win my "Crossed Guns" as a marksman at a later stage.

Being the only one to fire on the range that day, no facilities were laid on for boiling water, the accepted method for cleaning out rifles after a shoot. I was told to try the mess kitchen. The water was only lukewarm when I called and as I tried to remove the internal fouling in the barrel, someone called to me that I was due to parade for guard duty that evening. This meant I had to rush to get ready – all kit and equipment had to be spotlessly clean, boots and bandolier and all brass tunic buttons were expected to shine like glass. In the rush I did the best I could to polish the barrel of my rifle but it refused to shine without the boiling water treatment. The result was, as luck would have it that the Scots Regimental Sergeant Major was on guard parade and on the command "Port Arms", I suddenly had a feeling that he was going to peg me that evening. On the command "For inspection, examine arms" I carried out the movement smartly, but when he glanced down my barrel and saw the dullness of the metal, he gave me a look of condemnation. "Your rifle is dirty, mon! You parade at the Commandant's office tomorrow at 9 a.m." I was on "the peg".

To make matters worse, when it was my turn to take up guard duty at the stables, I got into more trouble. I went around all the stables, being the first of the four to take guard, and found all the horses well tied up and quiet, with most of them sleeping on their feet, as horses are accustomed to do. I was tired from the day's exercise and when I discovered a bale of hay I decided to sit down and rest a little while. What happened on that bale of hay I shall never know! All I do know was being prodded in the ribs by a red-faced RSM who did not mince his words or adjectives when he found me asleep on duty.

This was the second charge he had against me in just a couple of hours so you can imagine my feelings about what was in store for me at nine o'clock the next morning. I visualised a spot of hard labour in the Salisbury gaol! Imagine, therefore, my surprise the following morning when I was paraded and marched before the Depot Commandant. Having read the charges, to which I pleaded "guilty", this red-faced Scotsman stepped forward smartly, "Permission to speak, Sir." The Commandant nodded his assent. The grand old soldier, in a speech he must have used on numerous occasions, pleaded on my behalf.

"This man is the finest recruit we have in Depot – I really don't know what came over him, Sir, but I do think a caution would meet the case on this occasion."

"Duly cautioned," agreed the Commandant.

Then the RSM took charge: "One pace step back, march! Salute! Rrright turrn," in his broadest Scottish burr. And as I got outside the Commandant's office, "Halt! Now look here, mon, I do not want to hear any more of this dirrty rrifle on parade nor do I want to see more of sleeping on stable parade – is that quite clear?"

"Yes, Sir."

"Right turn, dismiss." And that was the end of the matter. Never again was I caught with a dirty rifle or asleep on stable guard!

I was fortunate when I was allocated my first riding horse. He was Number 1488, "Charcoal". Later, by his transfer to Gwanda as the District Superintendent's mount for the tent pegging events in the Gwanda gymkhana, he came back to me and remained in my charge for the duration of my stay in the Force. By the layman, "Charcoal" would be termed a black but in Police official records, he was classified as "brown" because his muzzle was brown in colour and this is how the "colour" of a horse is determined.

The riding school and ménage, the jumps and the animal management lectures were comparatively easy for one who had ridden along bridle tracks in Basutoland for many years so I soon won my spurs. In fact, my half-section, Jack Cornwall, and I were the first to win our spurs in the squad. And, later, when we were put to riding remounts, Jack and I were given the two most jittery horses to ride. Consequently we were the last to get mounted. This was common procedure where remounts were concerned, adopted in case the jittery horses upset the tamer ones by their unpredictable behaviour. I remember one morning in particular, Jack had successfully managed his horse "Smoke" and I was told to bring mine up into the line. His name was "Boots", named as such by a recruit who was employed by Boots, the London chemists, before joining the B.S.A. Police.

As I swung my right leg across the rear arch of the military type saddle we were issued with, "Boots" suddenly leaped forward and the baggy part of my riding breeches became hooked on the rear arch. The lurch forward caught me badly balanced with my left foot in the near-side stirrup as my only support. My right foot was jerked back towards the horse's tail and the spur became lodged above the tail. This foreign object poking him on the rump was more than enough to make any self-respecting horse pig-root and buck.

"Boots" seemed to have only one thought in mind and that was to get me off his back. With a series of short sharp bucks he was through the line of horses and in the open square where the RSM and one of the sergeant-major rough-riders were watching proceedings. Here in the open "Boots" gave vent to his hurt feelings. His head went down between his knees and he bucked continually in his efforts to dislodge me. Fortunately, the stirrup leather held, otherwise I would have been forcibly deposited on the hard gravelled ground. I was unable to see where I was going – my cap had been jolted over my eyes. But I could hear the sergeant-major rough-rider saying in rather a loud voice, "Watch where he settles!" This was a favourite phrase in the riding school when recruits were being put through their paces. It was coined when a Rhodesian Member of Parliament, advocating the recruitment of policemen from England, observed: "... and then once their contracts are completed, watch where they settle."

The RSM was bellowing for me to look out for his trees. These too had a history. They had been planted by the RSM when he was serving time for desertion from the Police at the outbreak of World War One. He had tried unofficially and unsuccessfully to rejoin his old regiment, The Scots Greys, in 1914; had been arrested at the Railway Station in Bulawayo after leaving his station at Gwelo without permission, and after something of a minor legal tussle, had been sentenced to a period of hard labour in the Depot. Much later he had returned, all forgiven if not forgotten, to become the most important man in the training school. His pride in his lemon trees can be easily understood.

Meanwhile, "Boots" was ploughing through those same trees. Luckily my cap took the force of the impact with the branches from my face and also pushed back my headgear so that I could see where I was going. I managed to grab the reins and, still balanced on one foot, gained some sort of control over my mount. We returned, more soberly, to join the ranks, "Boots" making one last effort to protest at his treatment by giving a tremendous buck. I felt my riding breeches rip open at the seam caught on the rear arch of the saddle, and the next second, with my right leg freed, I was sailing through the air to land on both feet next to the horse's head.

With the threat to his precious lemon trees removed, the RSM's relief was secondary to mine. He uttered one of his few words of praise as I scolded the horse, led him to the rear of the line and mounted without further fireworks.

By the time we had mastered the education of the remounts, we were nearing our own time of departure for the outside districts. We were given forms to fill in and I chose the Gwanda District, chiefly because my cousin Mick had spoken so highly about it. Others chose districts in Mashonaland but no one really knew where he would eventually be transferred or when such an event was likely to take place. To take up time and keep us occupied we were given foot drill, allowed to join the cricket or boxing team and, on rare occasions, were permitted to follow the hounds on a Sunday morning. The drill periods provided further chances for the RSM to let off steam – he was a terror as far as the staff clerks were concerned, loved to get these chaps on parade with rifles and give them a session of arms drill, such as only he could administer.

On Saturday morning he had them out after inspecting their barrack rooms and, not being satisfied with their performance, ordered them to fall in again after eleven o'clock tea. One individual resembled Billy Bunter, the fat boy depicted in so many school boy yarns and, as the bugle for "Fall In" sounded, he was stretched out on his bed recovering from the earlier parade. In haste he tightened the belt he had loosened when flopping onto his bed, grabbed his rifle and came out at the double to fall in with the others who had already lined up at the "at ease" position. The RSM was there waiting for him and immediately caught sight of the kingfisher blue silk pyjamas Billy Bunter had unknowingly attached to his belt. The pyjamas had followed him on to the parade ground. The RSM's face grew redder and redder. Finally he bellowed: "Billy Bunter – you at the end – two paces forward, march!"

There was a burst of laughter from the rest of the assembled squad as the RSM yelled: "Now file away and take those damn silk pyjamas off your belt – at the double!"

One day soon after this the members of No. 8 Squad were told that we would be sitting our passing-out examinations the following day. There were papers on Law and Police work and animal management as well as practical exercises on horseback and arms drill. These completed, we were told that we had earned our passing-out parade and that the Commissioner of Police would be inspecting us on a certain day. It was up to us to put on the best show possible. There followed the usual spit and polish parade with all members of the squad taking a hand at polishing their kit and equipment. We all used the easy Brasso method to bring a shine to our tunic and bandolier buttons, our bridle brasses and saddle D's and, of course, we all had our special formulae of boot polishes to brighten up our boots and leatherwork.

Finally the day dawned and, with our horses groomed to perfection, we were all saddled and standing to our horses on the grass parade ground in front of the Commandant's office awaiting the arrival of the Commissioner. Our instructor "Tickey" was there putting the final touches to saddlery and bridles. The RSM was marching up and down the lawn, with leggings that had been boned and which shone like glass, his Sam Browne glistening in the sun and his swagger cane with its leather covered handle tucked under his arm.

As the Commissioner, who had risen from corporal to his present position, stepped onto the lawn the RSM brought us to attention, saluted the Commissioner and with "All present and correct, Sir" turned and followed the Commissioner, who had acknowledged his salute, towards the squad drawn up for his inspection. Here "Tickey" reported "No. 8 Squad ready for your inspection, Sir", saluted and fell in behind the RSM. Thus the inspection took place and as far as I can recollect little was said but the Commissioner did ask one question. "Mr Douglas, what do these men use to polish their brass-ware?"

I imagined he asked this question on every passing-out parade he undertook for the answer came without hesitation, or effort: "Oil, bath-brick and old sock, Sir."

I am sure that both of them knew full well that everyone of us, including the RSM and Commissioner, used the tinned metal shiner and never resorted to the ancient method of oil, bath-brick and old sock!

The inspection of horses and men over, we were given the command to mount. We then moved around in sections and half-sections at the walk, the trot and the canter, to show off our paces. Finally we were drawn up in line to receive an address from the Commissioner. It went like this:

"You men are now about to go to your districts and there you will be expected to go on patrol. There is one point I want all of you to bear in mind. Remember your horse and your pack animals travel best in the early morning. It means early rising and I want to see the right leg of every one of you swing into the saddle as the sun touches the horizon. Let your patrols be Sunrise Patrols. That is the best advice I can give you. Now carry on, Mr Douglas."

CHAPTER TWO

To Bloemfontein

Our pass-out parade over, we were destined to await a posting to one of the districts. It could be as much as a month before each of us received his route instructions and during the waiting period we still had to turn out for Depot parades. Having been through "the mill" however, the parades were merely time-filling exercises and as "trained men" we were spared the humiliation of doubling around the square with fixed bayonets. We were now policemen and ready to do our duty in one of the far-flung outposts of the British Empire!

New recruits were flooding into Depot. Two in particular – one an Irishman, the other a Scot – burst onto the scene just as we were anticipating our release from the confines and disciplines of Depot. Both of these new recruits had been tobacco farming until the sudden slump caused them to seek employment elsewhere. They were accepted in the B.S.A. Police and became room-mates during their training.

What happened on that one very eventful night was never quite clear to those of us in Depot.

My half-section had borrowed a book from the Irishman that evening and was as surprised as the rest of us to discover the next morning that the Irishman had been murdered by his room-mate. The Scotsman had stuck a military bayonet through the victim's shoulder and penetrated the heart. There were various reconstructions of what followed. One version was that the Scotsman then grabbed his own bayonet and had tried to commit suicide. A more hazy and curiously unsubstantiated theory included a second potential victim who had given the Scot a black eye the previous day – in attacking his second victim the murderer had collided with the door and injured himself with the unsheathed bayonet. What was not in doubt was that the Scotsman had suffered a nasty gash in the stomach resulting from an upward thrust of the bayonet – and that he was now in hospital.

Our squad was detailed to guard the prisoner who, being

deprived of anything sharp, grew quite a gingery beard which made him look much older than his true age. Eventually his wound healed and my half-section, Jack, and I were detailed to make up an escort together with a corporal and convey the Scot to Bloemfontein. There he was to be placed in the mental asylum, there being no such institution in Rhodesia at that time.

On receiving our orders, I immediately wrote to my father in Basutoland, asking if he could possibly make the trip to Bloemfontein to meet me. This proved impossible as I was to find out in a long letter from my father which reached me much later in rather a strange manner.

The train journey south was uneventful. Our prisoner behaved himself and made no attempt to escape. He busied himself drawing pictures of trains and steamships in a child's drawing book he had acquired while in hospital and before we parted he presented his drawings to me. On close examination I realised that he had used the same pages over and over again, rubbing out his first drawing and replacing it with one and sometimes two fresh attempts. His express trains and steamships followed a single pattern without variation and once you had seen one, you had seen the lot. He made no attempt to draw his favourite subjects from a different angle and I gained the impression that he had started on his theme as a child – of, say, eight years old – and that although his body had grown his mind had remained that of an infant. His conversation was normal but we thought it best to say nothing of the trouble he had got himself into nor was any hint given of his final destination. On reaching Bloemfontein we hired a taxi and went straight to the asylum where the unfortunate Scotsman was expected. Jack and the corporal took him inside while I remained at the door. I wasn't sorry. Jack later confided that if the Scotsman was not insane before his admission – just a little simple – he would soon become as unbalanced as the rest of the inmates.

A more cheering post-script was that we later heard that he had been released about a year after his admission and sent back home to Scotland.

With our duty done, we were at liberty to relax and enjoy our stay while awaiting the next train back to Salisbury. We booked in at one of the hotels and I imagine we created something of a stir – three smartly-dressed khaki-clad young men signing up for bed and breakfast. The manager/owner of the hotel made us most welcome and so did his comely daughters who, it so happened, were that night attending a swimming club ball in the city. It required little effort on their part to persuade us to join their party – despite the fact that we were wearing riding breeches, puttees and even spurs. Explanations of our presence – and garb – caused us to be introduced to most of Bloemfontein's leading citizens who warmly welcomed us. Amid all this hospitality we thoroughly enjoyed ourselves, doing the Charleston up and down the polished dance floor with a "bevy of bathing belles" from the swimming club lining up to partner us.

In the midst of all this hilarity, the blue uniform of a member of the South African Police appeared at the main entrance. He caught the eye of our corporal and beckoned to him. I noticed them in conversation and then the corporal came over to me and said I was wanted by the policeman. A little worried I did as I was told.

"Is your name Palmer?" asked the policeman.

"Yes, it is," I replied.

"Do you mind coming along with me. I want a word with you."

I followed him down the steps of the hall, wondering what he was feeling for in his inside pocket. Had he a warrant for my arrest or a summons? As we reached a quiet, sort-of-confidential spot in the street, he produced a letter from his pocket. Quickly I recognised my father's writing on the envelope. But before I could say anything, the policeman spoke: "I'm terribly sorry, but I opened your letter as my name happens to be Palmer too. It arrived at our mess and I thought it was from an old friend. Of course, when I read it I realised my mistake and all evening I've been trying to trace you."

"Anyone could have made a similar mistake," I replied, very relieved that the rather sinister approach had no more serious consequences. I explained what we were doing in Bloemfontein, told him again that his opening of my letter had been a perfectly understandable mistake, shook hands and the two policemen Palmer parted.

When I returned to the dance both Jack and the corporal immediately demanded to know what was up. I explained, waving my father's letter in which he apologised for not being able to get to Bloemfontein at such short notice.

The tremendous hospitality we had received made Jack and I persuade the corporal to apply by telegram for a few days' leave

– not that he needed much prompting. The request was unfortunately turned down and we were obliged to board the train the next day. So ended our very pleasant excursion in South Africa – a "duty" very much envied by our colleagues back in the Training Depot. Unfortunately I was denied the pleasure of telling the Bloemfontein story to the rest of the squad. In Bulawayo a telegram from Police Headquarters told me to proceed direct from Bulawayo to Gwanda which was to be my first posting.

CHAPTER THREE
Gwanda

The sudden transfer to Gwanda on my way back from escort duties to South Africa left me little time to make arrangements about my kit which was still in Salisbury. Fortunately Jack, my room-mate who had also been on the trip to Bloemfontein, knew where to find most of my possessions. He would also look after my puppy, Judy, a sister of Jack's pet, Trixie. (Jack had earlier arranged to take the two pups of a litter, knowing full well that I would be delighted to have a pup of my own.) Before I left Bulawayo for Gwanda, Jack promised he would personally make sure all my kit and equipment and my rifle were loaded on the train from Salisbury and personally escorted by Judy to Gwanda.

At Gwanda I was soon made at home because the policeman on station duty was a Depot acquaintance of Squad 7/27 and we were able to exchange local and Depot news.

Gwanda Police Camp of those days was not an immediately attractive sight. At the base of a steep hill, it had been built on rock foundations and there were no gardens or lawns to soften the bleak appearance of the place. The barracks were very solidly constructed of stone – they had been built to double as a fort and no bullet could have penetrated the thick walls. But by the same token the window spaces and the narrow doors left much to be desired, particularly on hot still nights. (It was not long before I joined those who preferred to sleep on the earth floor of the veranda on the east side of the building with our mosquito nets slung from the beams.)

There was a cone-shaped kopje – Mount Cazalet – overlooking the camp with its crown of cliffs and scrub trees stretching down to the base to border on the gymkhana ground. The distance to the top of Mount Cazalet from the barracks was roughly three-quarters of a mile, the vertical interval being some 1 400 feet.

One Sunday morning after a night shower of rain the mountain stood out so clearly that I expressed a wish to climb it. Several of my companions who had made the climb tried to dissuade me by saying how long it would take. "At least an hour," reckoned one of them who was nicknamed "Corks".

"Nonsense," I boasted, "I'll reach the top and be back in twenty minutes."

"Five bob says you don't."

"You're on," I replied, sealing my bet with Corks.

On the peak was a survey beacon, on the metal plate of which I was to sign my name as proof of my achievement.

At ten o'clock I set off in shorts and tennis shoes with a stub of pencil in my pocket as my mess-mates strolled back to the quarters in anticipation of their eleven o'clock cuppa. The climb was more strenuous than I had anticipated but I kept at it and eventually reached the top from the eastern approaches in good time. Having scribbled my name on the metal beacon plate, I looked around to get my bearings and it came as something of a shock to find that I had moved around the mountain. Instead of the Police camp being at my back where I thought it should be, it was directly below. It was just as well that I had checked my position before the homeward dash.

I had planned on a straight line back to the camp but no sooner had I started than a rustle – to my mind of a large reptile – beneath the fallen leaves on a crown of rock ahead made me change course. I had no wish to cross the path of a browsing black mamba or python. I chose a less-perpendicular descent and, as I slithered down a cliff face using a tree growing alongside as a ladder, there was a terrific crashing of deadwood beneath me and a great kudu bull broke cover and went bounding down the mountainside. This was a spur to my efforts and as the kudu shot off in one direction, I bounded over boulders in the opposite direction – hopefully away from other wild animals and reptiles. Soon I was through the tall trees that had obscured my view of the camp and was pleased to see that I had completed my descent to the edge of the gymkhana field. From there to the barracks was only a matter of 250 yards and I soon covered this distance. As I entered the barracks there was not a soul in sight. I flopped on my bed to catch my breath after the mild ordeal – my face was red as a beetroot and perspiration was dripping down from my hair. I grabbed a towel and was busy rubbing myself down when I heard footsteps and then voices on the veranda.

"Time's up – he can't make it!"

Having condemned me, the group came into the barracks to

find me sitting on my bed. The look on their faces was almost worth the five shillings I had won. There were, however, those who doubted that I had actually reached the top in the stipulated twenty minutes so I had the further satisfaction of watching a few of them make the climb that afternoon to examine the beacon plate. Corks paid his dues when they returned having found my signature.

"But it was very shaky," muttered one of the doubters.

In due course Judy and my kit arrived from Salisbury and I was all set to undertake my first patrol along the Insiza River in the company of my fox-terrier pup. I was allocated an old horse called "Mack" and for a pack animal I had been instructed to take "Rob Roy". This horse had been boarded for some reason or other – although there was no obvious cause – and the farrier-corporal was most insistent that he not be ridden. Rob Roy was dangerous, I was told. He would fall with anyone on his back. Having set out on patrol, I very quickly discovered that Mack was a most uncomfortable mount and as soon as I was clear of the camp I changed horses. To my delight Rob Roy gave me a beautiful ride.

I reckoned that Rob Roy had been badly misjudged and early one morning when a bush fence barred my way, I put him at it. He enjoyed the experience as much as I did. He put his ears forward and sailed over the fence without hesitation. True, he was inclined to stumble now and then but by riding him up to the bit I found he hardly faltered at all. There and then I made up my mind to ask the farrier corporal if I could ride Rob Roy in the forthcoming Gwanda gymkhana. The answer was a definite no. Denied the chance of joining in the fun of gymkhana practice and finding little pleasure in watching others rehearse, I volunteered quickly for another patrol.

My route instructions took me this time to Lumane Siding and early one morning I arrived at a dip tank in the area where the European supervisor was awaiting the arrival of some African-owned cattle. I was offered a cup of tea and while we were chatting he showed me a lassoo he had made from reims – raw-hide thongs. He explained that some of the cattle were shy about entering the dip tank and that it was sometimes necessary to round them up in true Wild West style, lassooing them on the run. I half suspected my leg was being pulled and asked for a demonstration. There was a convenient tree stump nearby. The dip supervisor was only too willing to show his skill.

Without fail he dropped his noose over the stump several times in succession. I remained sceptical.

"That's a piece of cake," I scorned. "What would happen if you practised on something live and kicking?"

There was a pair of kudu horns lying nearby. I picked them up, held them against my forehead and let out a bull-like bellow.

"Let's see how you do with a moving target!"

With that I galloped towards him, bellowing like a mad steer. He neatly side-stepped my charge and, as I sped past him, he cast the lassoo with such accuracy that it fell over the horns and caught on my shoulders. He then tugged on the wide noose which tightened over my buttocks, effectively trussing me up like a turkey ready for the oven. I let go of the horns and lay on the ground, well and truly nabbed.

Perhaps it was a fluke but the supervisor had certainly demonstrated his ability at my expense. By this time he was so helpless with laughter at my predicament that I could only join him in his amusement. So much for his home-made but very effective lassoo.

I spent nearly a week on that particular patrol before returning to Gwanda to report. By this time, the village could think of nothing but the planned gymkhana.

CHAPTER FOUR
Relaxation

The village was all agog with excitement at the forthcoming gymkhana and the ball that was to be held in the railway goods shed. It was to be a fancy-dress ball and the whole district promised to be present. Police units were riding in from outlying posts and numbers of people were expected to come from Bulawayo. The great day arrived and crowds flocked down to the gymkhana ground to see the field events. Whilst everybody was standing around or sitting in their cars to await the opening by the local District Commissioner, one tall fellow in Police uniform rode on to the field. He had just arrived from Filabusi and to herald his arrival let out a "Whoopee" and came galloping on to the ground scattering officials in all directions as he put his rather miniature pony to the jumps. But what a beautiful seat he had and what a game pony he rode. I later found out that he was Jock, ex-Scot's Grey's, and the game little horse was "Gnat". What amazed me was that the jumps were being taken from the wrong side – back to front – with the wings on the side the horse landed. Yet little Gnat never faltered but sailed over all he was put to.

The tent-pegging was the first of the horse events and I had the audacity to introduce myself to this gay fellow Jock, mentioning that I was Mick Baldwin's cousin. This acted like a charm for Jock as Mick had been recruited in England and had come out on the same boat with a batch of others – all ex-army men, in 1919. I told him I had admired little and begged him to let me ride him for the tent-pegging event. He agreed and added, "You'll find he can run straight." Sure enough he was a beautiful animal for tent-pegging but the only trouble was that I had last handled a lance when I was a youth of sixteen and then it was only a few runs on a horse owned by a great friend who farmed near Umkomaas on the South Coast of Natal. But the style he had imparted I had learnt well and during my runs up to the peg I caught the eye of an ex-cavalry officer who gave me some encouragement by saying, "I like your style, young man!" But try as hard as I could, I could not get a "carry" but only strike after strike. There were four of us in the event and though I came fourth I at least had the satisfaction of playing a part, which was better than being a mere onlooker. The event was won by our D.S.P. on Charcoal and second was the farrier-corporal on Abe.

Other events followed and in the 100 yards I managed to beat all comers. There followed the most popular event which, due to the number of entrants, had to be run in heats. This was the sack race. Twelve of us entered the final and by this time I had developed a technique which stood me in good stead. By turning myself sideways I was able to leap in the air and with every jump I covered a yard or more by pulling the sack up with my hands so that it did not fall each leap. Having passed the turning point where so many came to grief, I was at the winning post whilst others were still sorting themselves out at the turning point.

After this event came the bareback wrestling and for this sides were chosen. I was mounted on old Mack and after the final whistle blew I was the only one mounted so our side won the event.

Then followed the jumping. Again I threw discretion to the winds and approached the D.S.P. begging him to allow me to ride Charcoal for the jumping event. He was quite agreeable.

"But, Palmer, you'll find he is inclined to rush the jumps."

I answered, "Yes, Sir, I rode him over jumps in Salisbury so I know his faults."

"Carry on then and the best of luck."

"Thank you, Sir," and off I sped to saddle him in the stables. Here I met the farrier-corporal who wanted to know who had given me permission to ride the D.S.P's horse. I replied, "Why, the D.S.P. himself." He seemed nonplussed and went off mumbling something to himself about the newly joined recruits being too full of themselves.

There were only three entries for the jumping event so it did not take long. Charcoal did very well in the second round but he nearly had me off his back in the first round when he fouled the top of the triple bar. However, as his nose ploughed into the soft landing earth I leant back and recovered from the fall as my feet struck the ground. The high-jump was the next obstacle and this he cleared with a foot to spare.

Abe was playing at his old trick of crab-walking but despite this he was taking the jumps clearly and eventually won the competition. Darkie came second and Charcoal last. Both Abe and Darkie had been practising for weeks so I was not disappointed at the display Charcoal had given with such short notice.

For the fancy-dress ball that night I decided to go as a parson. I managed to borrow a black waistcoat and a dress shirt collar. By turning these back to front and donning a white suit, a pair of sun glasses and changing my voice slightly I pitched up at the local goods shed where a band from Bulawayo provided the dance music. It was surprising how many of my colleagues were deceived, partly because a parson was in the congregation for a church service the following day and everyone I spoke to thought I was the padre and questioned me as to what time I would be holding the service. The big laugh came when I was introduced to the parson himself but he was well disguised in a huge false nose.

During the interval the Master of Ceremonies announced the names of those who had won prizes at the gymkhana. The farrier-corporal, who was the chief organiser of the gymkhana, admitted that he had pipped me by half a point for the Victor Ludorum Cup. How he calculated the points I never questioned. I felt he was entitled to the cup for all the work and organising he had done.

I had won the Victor Ludorum at College so the half point that I was short this time just goes to show how near I came to winning the laurels a second time, in spite of the objections I had met with.

How I got half a point was rather amusing. The last event of the day was the cigarette and tie race for which one had to have a partner. It was this fact that caused the split point for the winning couple.

The dancing continued to midnight but I was too weary to see it through to the end and retired soon after the interval.

Thus ended a most pleasant and enjoyable occasion.

CHAPTER FIVE
My First Game Case Conviction

One weekend, an African named "Sout" came in to report that his master had not paid his wages for three or four months. I was detailed to take a statement from him and during the course of taking the statement, Sout mentioned that he had been out hunting with his master's son who had shot and killed a sable antelope. A check with the local Magistrate's Office proved that this young man had no licence to shoot "B" class game, so I was detailed to investigate the matter.

Leaving at sunrise the following day, I proceeded on horse and pack mule with a Native Constable, my private servant and witness Sout, to the scene of the shooting, which was near a ganger's cottage some 15 miles from Gwanda. This was the first case I was to investigate where Europeans were the culprits, so there were many words of advice offered before I left. I was told to be most careful, particularly as the daughter of the house was one of those most obliging young ladies who was looking around for a would-be husband and was not beyond trying fair means or foul to hook the unwary young man. There were stories of one young policeman who accepted a cup of coffee and became so ill after drinking it, that he had to spend the night at the cottage. Soon after this, the young lady fell pregnant and the young policeman was named as the father of her child – even before it was born. However, it was proved that others had visited her and the young policeman escaped the "hook".

On arrival at the cottage, I openly told them I was investigating both a case of non-payment of wages and one of shooting big game without a licence. Of course, Sout became the worst nigger in the land to them, but to me he was a first-class witness and during my search for evidence – no sign of which I was able to find at the cottage – he volunteered to show me where all the trophies and skins had been concealed. He led me to a spot in thick bush, where I found a large galvanised bath full of buck skins and perched on a stake, to act as a scarecrow, was an old hat belonging to the ganger's wife. This was the connecting link between the cottage and the scene. The hides were all from big game and were soon identified by Sout, despite the caustic solution that had been placed in the bath to remove the hair. Later, Sout took me to the spot where the sable had been shot and nearby I found the decapitated head with the tell-tale bullet hole right through the centre of the forehead. This proved beyond doubt that the young man was an excellent shot with a .303 rifle. I took the head along with me together with the skins, the bath and the hat but as it was late, I made ready my patrol tent for the night.

I was up betimes and called at the cottage to collect the wages for Sout. Suddenly a cup of coffee was pushed into my hand with the wages. I had made up my mind that I was not going to be caught out as had young George so I stood chatting for a long time, until someone remarked: "Why don't you drink your coffee before it gets cold?"

To this I replied: "I never drink coffee, only tea," and with that I passed the cup of coffee back to the young lady and mounted my horse to move on to my next place of call – which was the storekeeper, five miles away. There I watered my animals and later that afternoon moved back to Gwanda.

On arrival, I entered my report and eventually a summons was issued and the case against the young man came before the Magistrate. When in court, the accused was asked if he had any witnesses – he produced his mother. She climbed, with some difficulty, into the witness box and swore that she and not her son had shot the sable. However, the prosecutor produced the head of the sable and showed what a good shot had felled it. He then asked the witness whether she realised what a remarkable shot it had been over 200 yards distance.

"Yes, it was a good shot!" she agreed. "Now you say you fired the shot?" the prosecutor queried.

"Yes!"

"So you must be a very good shot with a .303 rifle?"

To this she had no reply and the case was closed with a fine – which was later paid by the old lady.

Thus ended my first game case with a conviction, thanks mainly to Sout, my actual eye-witness to the shooting of the sable.

Sout also denied that his old mistress had shot the buck. In fact, he had never seen her use a rifle while under her employ.

CHAPTER SIX

To the Limpopo

Whether it was the successful investigation of my first poaching case, or a report put in by the N.C.O. in charge of Mtetengwe police post, suggesting that a special game ranger patrol the banks of the Limpopo to apprehend game poachers from the Union side of the river, I shall never know.

But I do know that I was detailed to proceed to Mtetengwe and thence to the Limpopo, where I was to patrol up and down the river on foot to track down, wherever it occurred, the habit that the farmers and residents of Messina and its vicinity had, of crossing the river to shoot big game, which they carried back across the river on the backs of donkeys. Mtetengwe was a temporary post built of pole and dagga huts, with grass thatched roofs, and was situated about 28 miles from the Limpopo river which, in the winter months became a mere stream flowing through the heavy sand. I was expected to make this post my headquarters and all reports were to be filtered through Mtetengwe to Gwanda, the headquarters of the district.

I was instructed to leave all police kit and equipment at Mtetengwe and to proceed on foot, carrying only the bare necessities to the Limpopo. There I was to set up camp, and the more unofficial I made it look, the better – I was allowed to carry my revolver, provided I kept it concealed. I dressed in the most hobo-looking outfit that I could muster together and set off one May morning with two Native Constables – Tshalibana and Sifunye – who were also dressed in plain clothes. May made for hot trekking and the further south we travelled, the hotter it became. We rested for a couple of hours in the shade of some trees en route and finally reached the Limpopo late in the afternoon.

I chose the junction of the Limpopo and Umzingwane rivers as my camp site, mainly because water was available from either river merely by digging a hole into the river sand. A belt of reeds at the junction was cut in due course, to provide a wind-break and shelter from the sweltering sun. I was young – only 21 – and healthy, and looked forward to my two-three month sojourn on the Limpopo. The hardships that I realised I would have to put up with were more of a challenge to my improvisation than something to complain about. I missed my little dog "Judy" who I had left behind in the care of a colleague, because I realised that she would be very susceptible to wild game in the bush.

The day after arriving, I heard a shot fired in the late afternoon and on hurrying to the spot, found that one of the troopers from Mtetengwe had reached the Limpopo by some devious route and had shot a kudu bull to provide food for his retinue. He very kindly cut off a leg for me and my two constables, but by the time the cutting up was complete, it was too late to attempt getting back to camp, so I decided that we would have grilled kudu steak for supper and sleep the night on the banks of the Limpopo. A pile of brush-wood and a couple of logs soon provided a merry scene in the gathering darkness. I did not feel nervous, as the trooper had loaned me his 9.5mm rifle and a pocket of ball cartridges, while he continued his patrol up the river with his police issue .303 rifle. What remained of the kudu leg after our evening meal was put high in the fork of the tree under which we were to camp the night. I decided that we would take it in turns to keep watch and to keep the fire going throughout the night and elected to take first watch. Soon the two constables were sound asleep and I settled back with my pipe, to recall in my mind the events of the day.

I know not whether it was the strenuous walking of that day or the heavy meal of grilled kudu meat, but I must have dozed off whilst sitting at the fire. Something woke me and I found my pipe lying between my feet and the fire down to a few glowing embers. How long I had been asleep or what awakened me, I do not know, but I reached across to my right side and grabbed a handful of twigs which I threw on the embers. As they flared up there was a guttural growl above my head and on glancing up I caught glimpse of a full grown leopard – his mouth closed tightly around the remains of our left over kudu meat. As I dug my toes into the bodies of my two sleeping constables, the leopard came down the tree in a flash and bounded out of sight beyond the glow of the revived fire. Both constables leapt to their feet when I hissed "Ngwe" (leopard), grabbing their axes as I made a dash for my rifle. But it was too late and our meat had gone – the claw marks on the tree telling their own indisputable story.

None of us slept after that terrifying experience and perhaps it was just as well that the leopard had taken the kudu meat to satisfy his hunger and not one of us instead!

After the experience with the leopard, I exercised a deal more caution on the return trek to my base camp at the junction of the Limpopo and Umzingwane Rivers. On the way back I turned off the track in order to quench my thirst at a pool near the Rhodesian bank. It was there that I saw footprints of someone who had crossed from the Transvaal side of the river, wandered round a bit and then returned across "the border". There was no obvious evidence that this was one of the poachers I'd been sent on patrol to catch, but I had my suspicions. Before continuing my investigations, however, there were more important matters. After the previous night's fright, all I wanted was a cup of tea and a few hours' sleep.

The next day I dug out my most worn and tattered clothing and crossed the Limpopo to the Transvaal side. I hoped my "disguise" was enough to make my quarry think I was also a Transvaal resident! Eventually I reached the spot opposite the place at which I'd first seen the footprints and, with very little trouble, came across the camp of a European who was, if anything, dressed in clothes even more ragged than mine.

I addressed the man in English and got no response. Then I tried Sindebele but this too apparently meant nothing to him and neither did Sesuto which the Northern Transvaal Africans used frequently when not speaking Afrikaans. Finally I resorted to my very small vocabulary of Dutch to which the man responded immediately, greeting me with a guttural "Dag". From what followed I gathered that he was the representative of a German-based company which hoped to process into paper the numerous baobab trees in the vicinity – indicated with much waving of the arms. It was then up to me to supply some reason for my presence so I tried to get across the story that I had been commissioned to find toucan eggs for the Natal Museum. Why I chose such a cover I don't know, because not only did I have to pantomime the bird itself but also its habit of boring holes in trees in which the female lays her eggs and her subsequent captivity when the male patches the hole with clay, leaving only a small opening through which to feed his mate.

I think we ended up equally suspicious of each other but I retreated in the direction from which I'd come, assiduously studying the trunks of trees for toucan nests. The stranger's reasons for camping on the river were about as thin as the paper he hoped to make. But time would tell.

Back at my camp I thought the matter over and resolved that the native constables and myself would keep an eye on the suspicious character on the other bank. He seemed a very likely poacher.

While waiting for the suspect to give himself away, I decided to try out the old 9.5mm sporting rifle my colleague from Mtetengwe had left with me. His comment had been that the barrel was so worn that one stood little chance of hitting a haystack at a hundred yards.

Downriver from my camp I came across a herd of waterbuck drinking at a pool. My first shot was so high that it raised a cloud of dust about a hundred yards beyond the big male that I'd aimed at. All I'd succeeded in doing was stampeding the herd but the buck were a long way from cover and I was able to get in a second shot. This too went high and by the time I had reloaded only one fully-grown cow remained in sight. I fired at her feet expecting to see the sand spurt but, to my surprise, the cow ran a few more paces, coughed and then fell over stone dead.

Back at the camp I told the constables that there was plenty of waterbuck meat for the collecting and was somewhat surprised at their lack of enthusiasm. Later they admitted that it tasted like donkey-meat and I had to agree, but it was palatable in soup and stews and from what was left we made biltong.

It might have been the smell of the drying biltong which brought the leopard back into our acquaintance and a few nights later there was little doubt that it was him that was responsible for the noise like a giant saw tearing into timber as he prowled around the outskirts of the camp. When the sound became a nightly occurrence, it didn't make for happy dreams.

The climax came when a troop of baboons decided to sleep the night in one of the large trees growing on the riverbank. We heard them chattering away as they settled for the night. Then came the ominous grunt of the leopard, the noise coming closer and closer and putting an abrupt stop to the chatter of the baboons. Then there was complete silence apart from the chirping of the crickets in the reeds. We waited in suspense for what must have been minutes. And then absolute pandemonium broke loose among the apes and while we saw none of the action, it was easy to imagine exactly what was happening. There was a despairing shriek from the victim, almost as frantic shrill cries of alarm from the rest of the pack and then the deep bark of defiance from the leader. More squeals and then came the breaking of branches as the hunter bounded away with its victim between its cruel jaws. It took an age for the baboons to settle and their pathetic mourning kept us awake for most of the night.

It was then that the senior constable, Tshalibana, suggested that we hunt the leopard and, in a moment of weakness, prompted mainly by the continuing distress of the baboons, I agreed. I still had trouble suppressing the constable's enthusiasm until the next day and at dawn I awoke to find him polishing the 9.5mm rifle, all ready for the fray. After having a cup of tea, I strapped on my revolver and we were off.

It was a dull day with plenty of cloud which, although it was still very early, shielded us from the climbing sun. Perhaps because of the overcast sky I wasn't as enthusiastic about getting the leopard as were my companions but as soon as we picked up the spoor of the marauder, a degree of keenness returned. The trail took us across the sand of the riverbed to the other bank where there was a long banana-shaped pool.

A forest of reeds skirted the pool and beyond was a clump of trees, dense with intertwined branches and straggling monkey ropes, a veritable haven for a leopard. On the ground the thick undergrowth allowed neither man nor beast to approach with any sort of stealth. A very narrow track led through the reeds and buffalo grass towards the densest part of the clump – and there was fresh leopard spoor leading towards the gloom!

Before setting foot on the track I loaded the revolver and also the rifle which Tshalibana was carrying. Only then did we move forward, with a great deal of hesitation. Very soon we encountered tufts of baboon hair – another ominous sign. If the leopard had dragged its victim this far, it indicated that it had young to be fed. If this was indeed the case, we were acting very foolishly in walking into the lair – without even the assistance of dogs to give us warning of danger. A dark cloud moved across that part of the sky where the sun was trying to break through. The entrance to the leopard's lair looked darker than ever.

Slowly we advanced into the gloom of the thicket and suddenly my nostrils sensed the feline presence. The scent was so pungent that I halted abruptly, trying to peer into the darkness on either side of the track. But I could see nothing and the heavy cloud denied us the sun's light at this crucial moment. Discretion was by far the better part of valour and I signalled to Tshalibana to retreat, and had to repeat the gesture as the constable tried to penetrate the darkness ahead, seeking the cause of my decision.

Back at the riverbed in a position of relative safety, I tried to explain why it was madness to continue the hunt. Without dogs we had less than an even chance – much better to follow the native custom of trying to tree the leopard where there was at least the chance of a clear shot. My caution finally satisfied him and we returned to camp for a late breakfast. So ended our not-very-brave leopard hunt – without even a sight of our quarry. It was the wisest course of action, of that there was little doubt.

On the way back to camp we came across the half-eaten carcass of a kudu bull and the indications were that a lion had been responsible. A lion will eat the brisket of its kill as first course, once he has felled his victim. We told a family of Africans near our camp about the downed kudu and they set off immediately to collect the remains despite the fact that there were flies everywhere and the meat stank to high heaven.

While we had decided to postpone the leopard hunt indefinitely, the marauder was not so accommodating. He could be heard practically every night in the immediate vicinity of our camp. All that changed was that the baboons appeared to have learnt a lesson, they never returned to roost in the trees at the river junction.

CHAPTER SEVEN
My First Poacher

The sequel to our finding the half-eaten carcass of the kudu bull on the way back from our unsuccessful leopard hunt was that Tshalibana sought my permission to visit the nearby village that evening when we returned to camp. It was the meat he was after, I imagine, despite the fact that it was already stinking when we discovered it. I told him to be back before dawn but heard him return just after midnight. The next morning he was in a sorry state – as a result of the bad meat – so I left him in camp with a massive dose of Epsom Salts and decided to make a short up-river patrol alone. The other constable had been sent to Mtetengwe for supplies and to deliver my reports.

Shouldering the 9.5mm rifle, I left camp after my morning cup of tea, intending to investigate further the activities of the German "Baobab paper representative". Reaching the spot at which I had first come across the suspect's footprints, I deviated to get a drink from a pool and, in so doing, came across a fresh made-made trail leading into the reeds. Following the tracks deep into the reeds, I found strips of biltong hanging from a number of trees. I had some evidence now against the German – all I needed to do was catch him with the biltong or in the act of poaching.

I was busy counting the number of biltong strips when, completely without warning, there came the most bloodcurdling roar of the King of the Beasts only a few yards from me. I froze where I stood, straining my eyes into the reeds. With difficulty I caught sight of the head and horns of a waterbuck some twenty yards away. More concentration, with my heart pumping madly, showed me the twitch and switch of a blacktufted tail. I had disturbed Mr Leo at his dining-table and my one thought was to leave him in peace as quickly as possible. Foolishly, I had left the rifle next to the pool at which I had drunk.

Cautiously looking round, I saw a small mimosa tree to my right rear and decided to dive for the slim protection of this tree and then duck and bound from cover to cover to get away from the lion. The urge to make a less subtle getaway was strong but if I just charged away there was no way of knowing whether the lion was after me – until it was too late anyway!

Just as I was about to make my initial move, I chanced to see across the river six beautiful kudu cows, frozen like statues in midstride with ears cocked in a state of maximum alertness. They too had heard the lion's roar but had not my advantage of knowing exactly where the beast was.

A second roar brought me out of my wildlife reverie and, in gigantic bounds, I zig-zagged away from the predator. At a safe distance I looked back for the kudu but they had long since disappeared on the Transvaal side of the river.

I didn't stop running until I had reached the middle of the river. As I stood there waist-deep in the Limpopo with the midday sun blazing down on me and shimmering off the hot sand, I reckoned I was fairly safe. Hopefully, Mr Leo had feasted off the whole waterbuck and, with stomach full, was in the mood only for a siesta. I worked my way upstream in midriver until reaching the spot at which I'd stopped to drink, where I recovered my rifle. With the gun loaded, I felt a good deal safer and decided to take a rest myself. Finding a shady spot I took out my pipe and spent a few quiet hours watching the further bank for a glimpse of my German suspect.

At about four o'clock I gave up and set off on the four-mile walk back to camp. The track twisted and turned, with evidence of game on every side and after I had covered about half the distance, I turned a corner and came almost face to face with five kudu bulls who were apparently on their way back to thick bush after an early watering. The opportunity to bag one was too good to be missed and all I had to do was push forward the safety catch, take aim and fire. My target leapt into the air and fell stone dead. On examination I discovered that I'd scored a heart shot – at such close range even the much-maligned 9.5mm couldn't miss. I covered the kill with branches and marked the spot well so that the meat could be retrieved. I need hardly have bothered. Tshalibana, fully recovered from his stomach ache, had heard the shot and guessed that I had made a kill. He met me before I reached the camp, rejoiced at my news and asked if he could enlist the help of a friend at the kraal who had a donkey in recovering the carcass. Stipulating only that I wanted the kudu liver for supper, I left him to organise the retrieval party.

I made myself some tea and sat back, enjoying the prospect of a supper of fried liver. But it was not to be.

Too quickly, Tshalibana appeared on the scene in a breathless state. The hatchet which he had taken to carve up the meat was still spotless. It took him a while to recover his wits and the story he told could only have taken place on the borders of the great and greasy Limpopo ...

Tshalibana had found his friend in the village and made arrangements for two boys to follow them as they went ahead, eager to skin the kudu I had shot. They'd found my spoor easily, although the sun was low on the horizon, and at the spot where I had placed a branch across the trail nearest the dead bull, they discovered that someone had beaten them to the carcass. Two adult lions and four half-grown cubs were busy eating my supper and our fresh meat supplies for the next week! Tshalibana and his friend had got such a fright that they had returned to camp at top speed, thoughtfully stopping only to tell the two youngsters that their journey with the donkey was no longer necessary! Into thin air went my visions of liver and bacon for supper, but I was determined to check up on the story at first light the next day.

Later that evening the constable who had been sent to Mtetengwe returned to camp with bacon, potatoes, onions and tinned foods – some consolation for the loss of my supper. Tshalibana waxed strong over his companion with the story of how he had faced six lions with blood-dripping jaws. The story was a long time in the telling and eventually I had to send both constables to bed as there was much to be done the next day.

Tshalibana hadn't exaggerated. The following morning there was all the evidence necessary to show that the six lions had dragged my kudu from the spot where it had fallen and had gorged themselves very successfully to leave very little of the meat. There was more. Back-tracking on their pug-marks, it was evident that the pride had been following me when I shot the kudu. The prints in the sand went even further to indicate that the young cubs had pranced ahead of the adults and spied on my progress along the trail long before I'd encountered the kudu. It was as well I'd been unaware of my "spectators" but it proved that "where ignorance is bliss, Dame Fortune takes a hand". All sorts of possibilities went through my mind as I returned to camp. My second encounter with lions – had it materialised that day – would have meant, at best, a pride of lions wandering around the camp at night. It was fortunate that they had taken the bait I had provided so unintentionally and been diverted from a different menu.

Perhaps the liver and bacon supper wouldn't have sat too well after all.

CHAPTER EIGHT
Nineteen Mile Stretch

Proof positive of my first poachers was the snatching of my kudu bull – and a mouth-watering supper of kudu liver and bacon – from under my nose by the pride of lions that had followed me from the river. Having recovered from the shock of a narrow escape, my thoughts returned to the two-legged poacher whose biltong I had discovered drying in the trees along the bank of the Limpopo. Returning to the river the next morning, there were no new footprints in the sand so I instructed the two constables to gather up the biltong and take it back to camp – some compensation for our loss of the kudu meat. They quickly constructed a large basket which they filled with biltong and then slung on a pole before marching very happily back to camp.

Taking the rifle, I crossed the river to the Transvaal side to inspect the camp of the so-called German paper-maker's representative whom I strongly suspected to be the owner of the biltong. His camp site was deserted – perhaps he'd seen my footprints at the biltong cache and decided it was time he moved on. All I had gained was the biltong which came in very useful in supplementing our rations.

Over the next few days I planned my future strategy and decided to tackle the "Nineteen Mile Stretch", at the end of which I would enquire among the locals about the presence of poachers from over the border.

(Having gone to some lengths to identify the area concerned without success, we hope that a reader will be able to assist with pinning down the locality which the Author presumes was so well known in his day. His narrative confuses the issue later by mentioning that he and his companion had left the "river track" and, much later, that he came across a baobab tree "which should be declared a National Monument". It is most unlikely that he had travelled as far northwest as the "Pioneer Tree" on the old Tuli entry route, bearing in mind that his base camp was at the junction of the Umzingwane and Limpopo Rivers and that his parent police post was Mtetengwe, some 30 km due north of Beit Bridge. Can anyone assist, hopefully with a map? Editor.)

Tshalibana and I set off early one morning on foot with only a blanket each, some bully beef and biscuits and a water bottle. For protection – should we encounter more lion – I relied on the old 9.5mm rifle and half a dozen rounds of ammunition. We travelled light in order to cover the distance before nightfall! At first I was unable to understand why this established patrol had been named the "Nineteen Mile Stretch" until I became aware of the silence and the complete lack of habitation. It was a forgotten corner of the country where not even a cock crowed to herald the dawn.

The day was a scorcher and the track was sandy and so hot that it burned through one's boots. At about midday we shared the last of our water – it was lukewarm and unrefreshing. We had left the river track – as it had become heavier with every step we took – and were following a track into the hinterland where Tshalibana said he knew of an African kraal. By five o'clock there was neither sight nor sound of habitation in the stillness of the late afternoon. I was hungry and tired so we shared the bully beef and biscuits, after which I would have given my eyebrows for a drink of water. When I mentioned my thirst, Tshalibana took the empty water bottle, the rifle and the small packet of cartridges and said he would get water. Before I could raise a voice in protest, he was trotting down the track still confident of finding the kraal at which there was a well.

The sun set and I gathered firewood for the night ahead. We had stopped on a *dwala,* a bald granite outcrop, and though it had been hot during the day, I knew it would be bitterly cold at night. There I waited, scanning the valley below for the returning constable and his promised water. As the night got darker, I realised that something had gone wrong – but there was nothing I could do until morning. I prepared for a cold night, making myself as comfortable as possible with a small fire and my single blanket.

The increasing chill of the air did nothing to lessen my thirst and then suddenly came the "gra-gra-gra" of a prowling leopard from the shallow valley below. I "watched" the sound of the beast as he circled the hill and when he stopped I threw more wood on the fire and hoarsely shouted "voetsak", hoping to scare him away. If anything he seemed to come nearer and I began to wish I had collected more firewood in the last hours of daylight, enough for a braver blaze. Above all, I had to stay awake.

The hours passed as I fed the small fire, walked around the

small circle of light and threw my arms about in the effort to stay awake. While there was no further evidence of the leopard, I had no way of knowing if he had moved off or was just lying there, waiting ... Nature eventually took a hand and I must have dozed off. In the early hours I awoke with a start, my tongue thick and stodgy from lack of water. As I remembered my predicament I threw a handful of twigs on the barely smouldering fire and as they burst into flame there was an obvious crackling in the undergrowth and the obvious retreat of padded paws. I put the fire between myself and the threat until I realised the noise was receding and calmed myself down. To this day I know not what type of animal had been prowling around. It could have been the leopard – or perhaps a hyena attracted by the smell of the empty bully beef tin. The intrusion achieved one thing. I no longer felt at all sleepy but how I longed for a drop of water.

Later, towards the dawn, my straining ears picked up the leopard some distance away and, thankfully, the noise faded towards the west. First light came and I had a splendid view of the birth of a new day. Then a bee buzzed past my ear, followed by others of his swarm. A "go-away" bird flew to a mimosa and announced himself. After the long cold night these sounds were reassuring but it was some time before the significance of these early risers dawned on me. Rising stiffly from my blanket next to the fire, I slid down the granite hill and walked towards the mimosa from which the lurie had called. Two more birds joined the first who seemed to be wiping his beak on a small branch. Only then did the thought strike me – birds and bees need water. Was it possible that there was moisture in the little spruit beneath the mimosa tree?

From the top of the donga I looked down on a patch of wet mud in the centre of which was a large pug mark. And in the pug mark were a few drops of dirty water. The birds and the bees had shared with me their secret. I almost fell down the bank and then my mouth was sucking up the most delicious water I had ever tasted – I didn't mind that it was really liquid mud.

When I stopped to regain my breath, I was shocked to find a piece of impala skin and hair beneath the surface of the mud. I scooped with my hand and the whole decaying leg of the animal was revealed to my disgusted eyes. I felt like vomiting but the liquid mud appeared to have clogged my stomach muscles. It needed little imagination to guess what must have happened.

Perhaps during the last drought the impala had staggered to the mud pool – in much worse condition than I – and had got himself stuck in the mud where he had died.

I walked back to my hill and shortly the sun broke over the horizon. Looking down into the valley, I saw Tshalibana trotting along the track towards me with the water bottle. Without hesitation I stuck my finger down my throat, heaved up the polluted water and filled my belly with the cool liquid which the constable handed me. With this operation over it was time for explanations.

Tshalibana reported that he had been treed by a pride of lions the previous evening. Although he had retained the rifle, he had dropped the cartridges when trying to load the weapon. There he had stayed for the night with the lions prowling around beneath him. One female had even purred up the tree and sharpened her claws inches below Tshalibana's perch ... according to the constable!

Any anger I felt at his absence or doubt about his story, was diluted with the promised water. We continued on our way, heading back towards the river track. I resolved never again to risk a path leading away from the river unless I was sure it was more than a game trail leading to a waterless grazing area.

On our way up the river we came across a very large baobab tree. It should be declared a national monument for carved into the trunk were the names of many pioneers who had passed this way. There were also the names of many policemen, some of whom I recognised. Evidently I had reached the end of the "Nineteen Mile Stretch" and I celebrated by adding my name to the roll of honour. We had a bite of food in the welcome shade of the baobab and then pushed on to the kraal which Tshalibana promised was near. There we proposed to sleep before making our enquiries and returning to the base camp.

The country changed considerably after the baobab. Gone were the sandstone and granite outcrops and we were now on a well trodden footpath. A cock crowed and I knew Tshalibana had kept his promise and that we were close to the kraal. Then a magnificent sable antelope crossed the track in front of us and watched our progress from behind a bush quite calmly, with his white face tossing up and down as though he was trying for a better view of us and his tail switching at the worrisome flies. There was little point in shooting him as we would never have been able to take the meat back to our base camp but then I reasoned that a whole buck presented to the villagers ahead might make them more talkative on the subject of international poaching. I loaded the old rifle, took careful aim at the proud white face and fired. The antelope dropped where he stood and within minutes we were giving the good news to the village headman and he was arranging for the carcass to be brought to the huts amid great rejoicing.

After a decent interval I brought up the subject of poaching but learnt nothing of immediate interest regarding my own investigations. We were told, however, that my colleague from Mtetengwe had passed this way with his pack of donkeys and that he had caught a bunch of poachers from Messina higher up the river. The case, though it never reached court, had an interesting aspect.

The trophies and biltong taken by the gang from Messina were found on an island in the middle of the Limpopo and the argument, that the middle of the Limpopo was the true boundary between Rhodesia and South Africa, was pressed to the point that the island was virtually no-man's land. It was only a presumption – a good one but not proven – that the game had been shot in Rhodesia and cached in safety on the island after being carried there on the backs of donkeys, the tracks of which were much in evidence. The case had frightened off the wily Messina poachers but it was only later that I heard of this sequel and gained the satisfaction of knowing that our efforts against the poachers were having some effect. That evening I pitched camp at the base of a baobab tree near the river and grilled some steak from the sable I had shot. Of course, our camp fire attracted many of the villagers who came either out of curiosity or to pay their respects. But one young buxom belle was bold enough to enter into the company of young and old with other things on her mind. Tshalibana knew what she was up to and told her that her hospitality was not required. But still she hung around until Tshalibana lost patience and dismissed her in the bluntest terms. I breathed a sigh of relief and Tshalibana went up in my estimation.

The following day we returned to base camp, arriving home in the late evening. It had been a long, hot and not very productive trek and I was thankful to get back to a strong cup of tea, a good wash and brush-up and a leisurely meal before turning in for the night.

CHAPTER NINE
Crocodiles

The next day was Sunday and time for a good bath. Having shaved and with a good breakfast beneath my belt, I grabbed a couple of towels and some soap and walked down to the Limpopo to where some large boulders formed a shallow pool. Undressing behind some reeds, I dived into the water, emerged and proceeded to soap myself from head to foot. With a good lather built up, I dived back into the pool. The bath made all the difference and as I dried myself vigorously, I stepped towards a larger boulder which would make the towelling process less precarious. It was then that I saw the tail of a huge crocodile slipping into a larger and deeper pool right next to the one in which I had bathed. What amazed me – apart from the presence of the predator – was the smooth and silent progress of the huge thing as he slipped out of sight, scarcely making a ripple in the pool.

Much later, when I was relating my narrow escape to an old native living in those parts, he told me of his own experience with a crocodile. He and his son had been at a pool washing themselves and he was in the process of rubbing his feet on a stone at the water's edge. The ugly head of a crocodile suddenly appeared and clamped its front teeth over one of the man's feet. He remembered some good advice about not struggling in such a predicament – this would only result in the croc dragging its victim into its more favourable element, the water – the man called to his son to bring him his hunting knife. With the knife concealed in his hand, he continued washing himself and as he reached his toe he rammed the knife between the crocodile's teeth and then, with an upward thrust, into the roof of its mouth. The assault caused the croc to open its mouth and release his leg and the native sprang to safety. Such presence of mind in the circumstances seems almost unbelievable.

A few days later, when I was on my way downstream through the "gorge" to report to the i/c of the Limpopo River Station, I came across a Nyasa sitting patiently on top of a large rock and gazing into the pools below. On questioning him, he told me he was trapping crocodiles. Seeing no sign of a net, I asked to see his trap. Going down to the pool I was shown a deep furrow leading from the water. As the trench stretched further and further from the water it became more shallow, stopping at a point at which a stout pole had been driven into the sand. To this pole, the man explained, he tethered a goat. The whole idea would be that the bleating goat would coax a croc from the river by way of the furrow. Once the beast was in the furrow he would be unable to turn around and the trapper would leap onto its back and despatch the reptile with a blow between the eyes from his axe.

I asked the Nyasa what he did with the skin and he replied that there was a ready market in Messina. Later I learnt that the trapper had started his career at his home in Nyasaland where there were many more crocodiles than in this part of Rhodesia. He also told me of a preacher who had been "converted."

This man had been casting his fishing net one day when he had been grabbed by a croc and pulled into a deep pool near the bank. There had been heavy rain and the pool was so muddy that one could not see beneath the surface. This victim was also aware of the good advice about not struggling and although his lungs were nearly bursting, he kept as still as possible. The crocodile must have been persuaded that the man was dead because the reptile pushed its victim well into the mudbank beneath the surface and let go of the leg. With his leg released the man looked up and saw a glimmer of light through the muddy water, light that could only be coming through a break in the riverbank. He kicked wildly for the patch of light and scrambled through what he described as a "Heaven-sent hole" finally collapsing when reaching safety. When the man had recovered from his narrow escape he offered up a prayer of thankfulness and later embraced Holy Orders, telling his congregation wherever he went of his near-miraculous deliverance.

A story nearer to home was that of two Mvenda women who were returning to Rhodesia having visited relatives in the Northern Transvaal. Crossing the Limpopo at its most shallow point, one of the women was seized by the foot by a croc and pulled towards a deeper part of the river. Her companion bravely hammered on the croc's nose with her bangled arm until it let go of its prize. The Mvenda women of course wear many copper bangles on their forearms and around their legs and in this case the rescuer's weapon must have packed all the punch of a four-pound hammer.

Before leaving this interesting foreigner, I asked him for a drink of water and he took me to his hut which was perched on the top of a kopje. There I was astonished to meet his wife who had a fair skin and fair but bushy hair. Her face was almost white and she had pale green, almost blue eyes. She could speak no English but was fluent in Afrikaans and I was wondering how she conversed with her Nyasa husband, when she asked him to bring a cup of water in Afrikaans. Despite her obviously mixed parentage, the woman was living as most African women do – even to the extent that there was a large bath of mud and dung in the hut and we had interrupted her in the process of plastering the floor of the building.

Later I learnt that her husband had formerly been a foreman at the Messina Mine – he was comparatively well educated – and that he had met his coloured wife there.

She was now sharing his retirement and the fruits of his labour as a crocodile hunter.

CHAPTER TEN
Limpopo Police Camp

After my interesting interlude with the Nyasa crocodile hunter and his coloured wife, I pushed on to the police camp at what is now Beit Bridge. There was no bridge in those days, of course, and if the river was in flood the drift could not be negotiated and travellers were forced to wait until the river subsided.

At the police station I had a long conversation with the trooper-in-charge. He had been in Messina recently and the town was full of the news that the Rhodesian police were carrying out anti-poaching patrols. This explained why I had experienced so little success in my own efforts to catch poachers – they had been warned off. While this was not very satisfying as far as I was concerned, it was good to know that the poaching patrols were having the desired effect.

I set off on my way back to camp and was rather surprised to come across a number of mining beacons which indicated that mining rights had been secured by the B.S.A. Company. Inspecting the nearby terrain more closely, I came across several nuggets of coal strewn about on the surface. I reached the conclusion that the coal must have been of low grade otherwise the railway line to Messina would have been extended these extra few miles to take advantage of the deposits. There was also the temptation to take back to camp a few of the nuggets to see how well they burned, but with so much wood about, such an experiment would be purely academic.

On my way back to camp along the Umzingwane I came across a herd of impala returning from water and mentally noted the spot at which they re-entered the bush. We had finished the confiscated biltong and some fresh meat would be most welcome. The next day I returned to the spot with my rifle and potted a large ram. This time my constables retrieved the carcass before lions got to my kill.

As I walked across the dry sand of the Umzingwane I distinctly saw Judy, my little fox-terrier bitch, run from the reeds to the camp waterhole which had been dug in the sand. It was almost as though she was looking for me and, on losing my spoor, had decided to return to camp to await my return. It was late in the morning and I hurried across the intervening stretch of sand to be re-united with my pet. On the way I explained to myself Judy's presence in this neck of the woods – she had fretted at my absence from Gwanda and some thoughtful person had brought her here. I was thrilled at such thoughtfulness but at the same time I had a few misgivings about the wisdom of bringing the dog to a part of the world in which there were so many predators.

When I reached the camp Judy had disappeared and when I asked the constables where she was, they just looked at me blankly. I got angry – I was so sure I had seen Judy at the waterhole – but still the constables denied her presence. No one had visited the camp. My heart sank with disappointment but at the same time I was relieved to know that I would not have the responsibility of feeding her and keeping her out of harm's way. But to this day I have never been able to account for the vision of Judy I experienced – was it a psychic phenomenon or just a mirage caused by the blistering midday sun.

What I do know is that at almost the same time as I "saw" Judy, a hundred miles away at Gwanda my little dog was running alongside a motorcyclist, was charged by a kaffir dog and was knocked under the wheels of the motorcycle and killed. When I heard of the tragedy I checked back and there was no doubt about the co-incidence in timing of my vision and Judy's death. Beyond this I cannot vouch for more. Nor am I prepared to suggest that man's best friend earns a heaven to which all faithful canines go.

The Rhodes and Founders holidays were approaching and I was told that all patrolling was to be stepped up as this was a popular time for Rhodesians to go hunting, fishing and shooting and was also a popular time for turning a blind eye to the game laws. I was out on one such patrol, travelling towards the Limpopo Gorge, when I heard shots being fired from a heavy rifle. Hurrying in the direction of the shots I was most pleasantly surprised to find four policemen of the Mtetengwe contingent who were shooting, without much success at crocodiles in the river. Others were trailing for tiger fish or fishing for bream. It was good to see white faces after a month or so of roughing it in the bush.

My colleagues congratulated me on my prompt appearance

after their shots and invited me to join them at their camp that evening. They were based higher up on the Umzingwane. I was most grateful for the invitation but after weeks of a spartan diet, my stomach was unable to do justice to the meal that was laid before me. Never have I seen such a spread or such a variety of tasty dishes laid on by the two chefs who formed part of this large-scale expedition. From *hors d'oeuvre* to biscuits and cheese and black coffee there was no let up. I battled valiantly and my reward was an almighty stomach ache which only a finger down the throat relieved. Fortunately mine hosts were spared of this spectacle of ingratitude as it was only when I was on my way home by moonlight that I performed the operation. Next day I stayed in bed late to recover from the effects of over-eating. My colleagues must have seen my lack of condition because a few days later I was recalled and told to report to Mtetengwe. As I packed up my things and struck camp, I was not sorry to be returning to a less-lonely existence.

CHAPTER ELEVEN
Mtetengwe

It was good to be back in civilisation, to have regular meals and enjoy a hot bath after my sojourn on the Limpopo. Little did I know that one day I would be returning to the same part of the country as the NCO in charge of the Beitbridge Police Station. After only a few days of leisure at Mtetengwe, however, I began to feel restless and asked that I be sent out on patrol again.

My pleas were heard and I was sent off to Liebig's Mazunga Ranch to check on some big game hunters who were reportedly taking a very heavy toll of the local wildlife. I was riding an old horse called "Trotsky" – a trot was about all one could get out of him, but he did have the reputation of knowing the lay of the land so well that he could smell his way back to camp on the darkest night.

There was the story of the trooper who went out on Trotsky to investigate a grass fire and lost himself. The horse tried to show him the way home but the policeman knew better and kept pulling the rein in the wrong direction. Eventually the trooper was so exhausted that he off-saddled Trotsky and, using his saddle blanket as protection against the cold and a small fire to keep predators from himself and his horse, he spent a most uncomfortable night in the bush. His fears were not helped by his mount's restlessness. Trotsky kept turning in circles and refused to settle down – giving the impression that he was agitated by the presence of a lion or leopard. This went on throughout the night and the poor trooper spent most of it walking around with his loaded rifle – until the first streaks of dawn showed in the east. Then and only then did the trooper feel safe and able to relax. Exhausted, he sat down next to a tree and fell into a deep slumber. He was awakened by the sound of the morning stable parade gong and was amazed to find his horse nowhere in sight. Picking up saddle and equipment, he dragged his aching body to the station where Trotsky was patiently waiting to be groomed. The trooper had camped down in the thick mopani scrub less than a hundred yards from his barrackroom bed!

At Mazunga I pitched camp while awaiting the arrival of my pack donkey with patrol tent and blankets. It was still only midday but I was told that the ranch employees made an early start at 6 a.m., working until 11 a.m. and then rested over a combined breakfast/lunch before recommencing work in the late afternoon. This timetable applied to the office staff as well so I was unable to "report for duty" and discover the latest information on the poaching until much later. In the meantime I was invited to the bachelors' mess where I met most of the junior European employees on the ranch. Over a cup of tea I listened to the stories they had to tell about life in this part of the world.

There was the legendary "Yank Allen" who had been employed to rid the ranch of numerous lions who were killing cattle by the dozen. He was reputed to have shot no less than 125 lions and his method was quite unique. He had a pack of about twenty fox terriers and the pack would put up the lion from its cover and worry the beast until it decided to stand up to its tormentors. Then Yank would wade in with a .450 revolver in each hand in true cowboy style firing from the hip and cocking his guns with his thumbs. The brave and nimble terriers would then set about the lead-filled lion until they had exhausted themselves. At that stage the lion and the dogs would be loaded into a van and be taken back to Yank's camp where rewards in the form of biltong would be handed out to the dogs for a good morning's work.

Then there was the story of the stockman returning to ranch headquarters on horseback one moonlit night. Suddenly his horse shied and there, right across his path, was a huge crocodile waddling from a dried-up haunt to a damper one on the Mzingwane River. The man leapt from his horse and despatched the crocodile with his revolver before the latter waddled much further.

This was the first definite information I had received of the movement of crocodiles overland at night and it proved the wisdom of always inspecting a pool before watering your animal. A crocodile could unexpectedly be lurking there one morning after making a similar overnight journey.

I noticed that quite a few of the ranch employees "packed" a gun in cowboy fashion and also spoke with American accents. There was more than a touch of the "Wild West" about

Mazunga. The reason for the American influence made amusing listening.

Liebig's had cattle-ranching interests in the Argentine, as well as Rhodesia, and Head Office considered it a sound idea that employees should be transferred from one country to another in the interests of giving the professional stockman a broader education. The story of two such individuals is a chapter in itself.

CHAPTER TWELVE
Cowboys on the Rand

The broader education which the Liebig's Head Office inflicted in its wisdom on its employees came near to creating some international incidents. There was the case of the two American ranch hands who were transferred to Rhodesia. Whether the transfers were primarily in the interests of the individuals or whether it was thought that the "foreigners" could show Rhodesians a thing or two when it came to handling cattle was an argument in itself.

However, the two Americans duly arrived in Johannesburg on the train from Capetown, and were met by the secretary of the local branch of the international company. The latter was very much of an "office type" – short in stature, wearing pince-nez spectacles attached to a cord, and with very little knowledge of very rough and ready stockmen. Imagine his feelings on seeing two strapping six-footers stepping off the Capetown train, men who were cowboys from the crowns of their broad-brimmed stetsons to the high heels and golden spurs of their cowboy boots, with a pair of six-guns slung above the traditional leather, goat-hide chaps. To complete the picture, each man carried his ornate, silver-trimmed saddle and heavily embossed bridle together with a neatly coiled lassoo looped over the front horn of the saddle.

The Johannesburg representative greeted the two newcomers and must have winced as they shook hands. Hustling them into a taxi, he whisked them away to the local office before the crowd of curious spectators got out of hand. There the host managed to persuade the two Americans to leave their saddlery and baggage, promising to have their equipment at the station in time for the Messina train that afternoon. In the meantime the two tall strangers were free to look at the sights of Johannesburg. The spectacle of two Western "gunslingers" high-heeling it down the streets of Johannesburg provoked as much curiosity in the city in the early twenties as a similar parade would cause today. The visitors sought to escape their inquisitive followers and took refuge in a pub which displayed on its walls a collection of game heads and horns. After ordering a drink – whisky, no doubt – the pair wandered around the bar making witty comments about the various trophies. At this stage one of the hangers-on foolishly decided to "take the mickey" by imitating the disparaging remarks of the strangers in the same Texas drawl. The cowboys accepted the mimicry in good nature until they had completed their tour of inspection and returned to the bar for a second drink. One of them rolled a cigarette and lit it, whereupon the mimic, getting insufficient attention in repeating the gestures, nudged the cowboy's glass and nearly upset the contents.

"Say, Mister – you looking for trouble?" asked the stranger, whose good nature was wearing a little thin. The mimic immediately turned to a colleague and repeated the same question, at the same time nudging the cowboy's drink again and this time succeeding in spilling the contents.

The cowboy flushed with indignation, dropped his right hand and came up with a gun which he fired, whipping the mimic's handrolled cigarette from his mouth and shattering a bottle of wine on a shelf in the far corner of the bar with a single shot. There was an immediate exodus of the curious – so much so that they jammed the entrance to the extent that a policeman who, having heard the shot and was about to investigate, was bowled head over heels. The barman ducked behind the bar and yelled for assistance. The two cowboys, having rid themselves of a nuisance with no great harm done, continued to sip their drinks as though nothing had happened.

The policeman got to his feet in time to see the sharp-shooter calmly reloading his Colt and, asking no questions, dashed off for reinforcements. Returning with a sergeant and three colleagues, the police asked a series of questions which the cowboys answered politely, also giving the name of the local Liebig's man in whose "charge" they were. One police officer telephoned the secretary while the two strangers were marched off to Marshall Square Police Station on a holding charge of firing a weapon in public with a charge of attempted murder much in the minds of their custodians. Naturally the offenders had been disarmed.

At the Police Station, in the presence of a very perturbed little Liebig's secretary, the cowboys were warned and cautioned and the investigation continued. The accused were very open about the whole affair but had some difficulty in convincing the police that the shot which removed the cigarette from their tormentor's mouth had been a "bull" and not a miss from a shot at attempted murder. The sharp-shooter offered to give a further demonstration if the sergeant would be good enough to hold a cigarette in his mouth. The latter declined but eventually, when the seriousness of the whole affair had been diluted to its true proportions, it was agreed that the cowboys would demonstrate their shooting skill with condensed milk tins as targets.

A more good-humoured parade assembled on a piece of waste ground just beyond the city where the cowboys put on a first-class display – rolling one of the tins with successive shots from their revolvers and then capping that performance by keeping another tin in the air with repeated shots from their guns. The final scene had one of the visitors spinning his gun on the trigger guard and hitting the tin each time the barrel of the weapon lined up with the target.

The performance was successful in convincing the policemen of the cowboys' innocence, the trembling secretary paid an "admission of guilt" fine for the discharge of a weapon in a public place and he then ushered the two men to the station to catch the Messina train – before restoring his nerves with a double whisky in the station buffet.

The two cowboys arrived safely at Mazunga without further misadventures where they discovered that the local method of catching cattle for branding was, by their standards, rather primitive. It was based on the use of a forked stick, wielded by one of the African employees, with a reim looped around the fork. This would be slipped over the hind leg of the animal – much easier said than done – and then the catcher would hang on like grim death until the opportunity arose of passing the reim around the other hind leg. With the animal grounded, the tail could be whipped between the hind legs and the branding operation could get under way.

The cowboys showed how it should be done – lassooing the animal around the neck and then tripping and securing the legs with a deft movement of the rope. This method meant that twice the number of cattle were branded in a single day – until the two experts realised that they were doing all the work and asked to be sent back to the more equitable labour arrangements of the Argentine.

While this particular pair of cowboys represented neither the beginning nor the end of the "exchange scheme", it was a fact that almost every one of the ranch hands at Mazunga wore the American-style leather chaps, "packed" a revolver on his hip, wore a stetson-type hat and spoke with a Texan drawl. It mattered not that some of them had never been nearer to Texas or the Argentine than the docks at Cape Town.

Despite the artificiality of some aspects of life at Mazunga, there was seldom a dull moment – and even in the occasional quiet period there was always the fascination of hearing the tales with which the ranch abounded.

I was glad I had come to Mazunga Ranch.

CHAPTER THIRTEEN
The Eland Hunters

Fascinated by the tales of the "Wild West" told to me by the cowboys of Mazunga Ranch, it was not until late in the afternoon that I was able to interview the secretary and discover the truth about the alleged poaching of eland on the ranch. It was all quite above board. The hunters had actually been hired by Liebig's to reduce the eland population which was seriously damaging the grazing in some areas.

The hunters were presently operating on one section, where the eland strongly outnumbered the cattle, and had established a base camp there. An unusual aspect of the hunters' contract was that they had permission to capture live one eland for every ten they shot – they had some scheme for cross-breeding with Africander cattle. Liebig's had seen to all the necessary licences and permits so my journey had really been to no purpose. Before returning to Mtetengwe, however, I decided to pay a courtesy call on the hunters. It was too late to set off that evening so I pitched my tent and, bearing in mind the Commissioner's injunction when we passed out from the Training Depot, I was in the saddle at sunrise the following morning.

Late in a hot and dusty morning I reached a dried-up river bed where there were a number of water troughs. The troughs were, of course, empty but nearby was a large, two-man sand pump with pipes running from the machinery to the troughs. I was examining the pump – the first of its kind I had come across – when from a small hut I had not previously noticed emerged a very deformed native.

The poor man had no legs to speak of. What passed for his lower limbs were two boneless flaps of flesh, identifiable by the toe-like formations at the extremities. He covered the distance between his hut and the pump with remarkable speed, using his arms as crutches. I replied to his greeting and asked if I might water my horse but already he had anticipated my needs and had swung himself up on to a stone platform next to the pump.

It was only then that I noticed his tremendous chest and

shoulder physique, developed over years of manual pumping. My offer of assistance was brushed aside and I could only stand and admire the ease with which he overcame the handicap he had been born with. Eventually I asked to be allowed to work the pump but, as hard as I tried, I could not match the cripple's rhythm and ease of operating the machine.

Later I asked the pump attendant how long he'd been so employed. The answer was almost six years – on almost every day of which he watered over 300 head of cattle at this primitive well. Here was an inspiring example of a man overcoming terrible deformity and excelling at his particular type of work. When my pack animal arrived and that too had been watered, I gave the attendant a couple of shillings in appreciation of his hard work. He beamed with gratitude and remarked that now he would be able to buy himself some tobacco. As we moved off, a large mob of cattle arrived at the troughs and the last I saw of this human miracle was his massive chest heaving up and down as he faithfully got on with his work.

That evening I arrived at the hunters' camp and established myself a little distance away under some thorn trees. Having had a cup of tea and something to eat, I went across and introduced myself to the quartet. With some pride they showed me round their base from which stretched for hundreds of yards in each direction wire fences loaded with eland biltong.

There was a young zebra haltered to a chain. I was warned to keep clear of him but curiosity got the better of me. I thought I had judged the length of the zebra's tether with enough accuracy but what I had not taken into account was the youngster's cleverness in galloping to the end of the tether and then reversing and kicking out with the hind legs. The hooves just grazed my leggings and more from humiliation than from suffering any injury, I lashed him on the rump with the riding crop I carried. Thereafter the zebra showed a little more respect for the B.S.A. Police!

As I made my way back to the four hunters who were most amused at the way I had been tricked, I heard the sound of a native violin and was surprised to see the minstrel herding a fair number of young eland cows. The way in which the cows seemed to keep in step with the herdboy as they marched toward a kraal of poles for the night was most amusing.

In response to my enquiry, the hunters told me that they caught the eland by running them down on horseback until their prey tired. Then they were lassooed and brought to camp where, after a few days, they became quite tame.

"Do you catch zebra in the same manner?" I asked.

"No man," came the reply, "you just jump from the back of the horse and bite his ear. He thinks you're a lion and, man, he stands still!"

I didn't swallow this story but my disbelief when told then that there were thousand-strong herds of eland quite near the camp was shown up when early the next morning I clearly heard the sounds of the multitude feeding and then saw more eland in the blink of an eye than the sum of those seen on numerous occasions on my travels.

I asked if I might accompany the hunters on their foray and they were keen that I should join them. We set off for the grazing areas soon after the sun had risen above the horizon. My companions' horses were very obviously built for speed and when I mentioned this one of the hunters admitted that some of their mounts had been on the racecourse. Aboard old Trotsky I had little chance of keeping up with them when the fun began.

On the climb to some high ground I was told that the eland herd habitually grazed in the shallow valley over the tree-lined crest. Reaching the trees, final adjustments were made to saddlery and the hunters checked their rifles. During this pause I became aware of a continual rattling noise from the valley below, a noise I couldn't place. Enquiring, I was told it was the sound of horns clashing as the eland grazed in close proximity to each other.

We moved off and as we broke cover there was a sight I would never have believed possible. There were literally hundred upon hundred of eland grazing on the sprouting young grass of the valley. The whole valley was filled with the buck and as each vied with his neighbour for a more tempting clump of grass, their horns touched to set up the rattle which I had heard a quarter-of-a-mile away.

I sat on my horse admiring the sight of a lifetime – but not so the hunters. At a signal they swept down on the herd in extended order, scattering the eland in every direction into the surrounding belt of trees and bush. Two bulls set themselves up as victims of the hunt as they followed the line of a *donga* with two horsemen in hot pursuit. Then another remarkable thing happened. As the horses closed the gap, each eland bull in turn leapt over his companion's back – almost in mid-stride – as if to take cover from the threat. The grace of the eland retreat made me think what a pity it was to destroy such beautiful animals but I'd ample evidence of the tremendous damage the herd was inflicting on the veld. Somewhat sadly I turned away and rode back to camp for breakfast.

Later, when the hunters returned, I recorded details of their licences and permits. Their efforts – massacres that they might have been – were properly authorised and of no concern to the police. I heard later, however, that when the hunters applied to export the live eland they had captured, a local outbreak of foot-and-mouth disease resulted in permission being withheld.

Presumably their captives were freed.

CHAPTER FOURTEEN
Leopards and Lions

Back at Mtetengwe I spent a few days completing my report and, this done, was told to prepare for my return to Gwanda. I was not sorry as Mtetengwe had never been anything more than a temporary camp and its pole-and-dagga thatched roofed buildings left much to be desired. Indeed, the troopers' quarters had originally been denied gauze screening until one youngster had a hair-raising experience. One night he made his bed on the stoep of the hut in which he was quartered. The trooper's dog, for company or for comfort, curled up at his feet. Their sleep was abruptly halted when the trooper awoke for some reason or other, sat bolt upright in his bed and returned the gaze of a pair of baleful green eyes. One swipe of the leopard's paw scooped the poor dog into remorseless jaws and then the predator bounded off into the surrounding bush. There was little the trooper could do – there was no hope for his pet. Despite the unlikelihood of the predator returning after a satisfying meal of what was accepted as a leopard's favourite dish, the trooper loaded his rifle and maintained a nervous vigil until dawn. A few weeks later wire gauze was installed around the huts so that the men could sleep on their verandas in a degree of safety.

Soon after this the local Assistant Native Commissioner was out on a Saturday afternoon hunt – looking for a duiker or a steen-buck for the following day's lunch – and reached a spot on the Mtetengwe where high banks protected a dry-season stretch of pools and exposed river sand. As the officer topped the high bank to look down on the pools, he saw a magnificent leopard in the prime of colour rolling in the sand and grunting with pleasure as the rough pebbles scratched its back. The hunter quietly loaded his rifle and, as the leopard rolled on to its belly to complete its toilet by licking one paw, carefully aimed at the neck and squeezed the trigger. The leopard gave one convulsive twitch and lay still – the bullet had severed the spinal column. Closer examination confirmed that the beast was a beautifully marked specimen and seldom was such a trophy earned in "sitting duck" circumstances. The killing so near the camp gave rise to the supposition that this was the beast responsible for taking the trooper's dog, partially confirmed by the fact that no more dogs or goats disappeared after the shooting.

Predators become very bold when hungry, especially when they are too old to hunt in the normal fashion. Gwanda boasted the legend of a policeman who was returning there with the body of a colleague who had died of blackwater fever. In the course of this unenviable escort duty, the trooper had to spend the night in lion country and decided to protect the body with his patrol tent while he himself slept in the open next to a roaring fire. During the night he heard a peculiar sound and on investigating, caught a lion pulling the dead man from the tent. He snatched a blazing log from the fire and rushed towards the lion – sufficient threat to make the beast release its burden and retreat into the bush. Needless to say the trooper got no sleep for the rest of the night and the body eventually received a safe Christian burial at Gwanda.

Another frequently-told tale at Gwanda concerned the local dip supervisor's experience with a black-maned lion, such beasts being rare in this area which had more than its fair share of jungle kings. At the routine dipping sessions, all missing cattle had to be explained to the satisfaction of the supervisor. One cattle owner reported that one of his oxen had been taken by a lion and the official's response was to ask if the man had a trap. He had, so the dip supervisor told him to set it and then report the outcome.

The following morning an excited cattle-owner brought the news that he had caught a very big lion and asked the dip supervisor to come and shoot it. The official wasn't very enthusiastic – unusually he had nothing larger than a pistol with him. Asked if there was anyone with a heavier weapon, the cattle-owner admitted that he had a rifle but only one bullet! Having been brought the gun, the dip supervisor was hardly encouraged to set out after the lion. The old Martini had wasps' nests which had to be cleaned out before light could be seen down the barrel and the solitary bullet was of soft pliable copper which was literally green with verdigris. The dip inspector made up his mind that he wasn't about to risk his life with such tools.

He changed his mind when he was shown the lion caught in the trap. It was the first black-maned beast he'd seen in that part of the country and the "very big" lion would certainly make a prize trophy. The dip supervisor cleaned out the barrel of the Martini as best he could and then set about polishing up the single round. Not knowing whether the rifle fired high or low, right or left, the very nervous hunter resolved to get as near as possible to his target.

Crawling on his belly, the dip supervisor – whose name was George – wriggled from one tuft of grass to the next but was very soon detected by the trapped lion. At first the beast seemed puzzled, wondering why man – his arch-enemy – was creeping up on him so relentlessly. The trap was secured to a large log and all the lion could do to discourage George's approach was to lunge at the approaching hunter, his black mane fairly bristling with rage, before the trap on its front foot brought it up short to roars of pain and frustration. Some twenty metres from the lion, George decided that he was quite close enough, aimed at the broad chest as the lion paused before making another lunge and squeezed the trigger with a prayer.

The recoil of the rifle and a cloud of black smoke confirmed that the single bullet had fired. When the smoke cleared, the dip supervisor was relieved to see that the beast had collapsed and was lying motionless with only the wind stirring the heavy black mane. George drew his pistol and approached very cautiously. There was blood gushing from the lion's mouth, indicating a fatal heart or lung shot, but what sent shivers down George's spine was the manner in which the beast had been trapped! It had caught the lion by no more than one claw. Had the victim been a leopard, it would have chewed itself free.

There was great rejoicing among the locals at the removal of such a major threat to their lives and their cattle and they set about skinning the animal, under the dip supervisor's careful instructions, with a will. The bullet hole was neatly included in the cut down the centre of the chest and the trophy was as perfect as the most meticulous hunter could have wished.

George returned to Mtetengwe with his prize, initiated the tanning process and the skin and head were then left in a tree to cure. The story didn't end there. Soon afterwards, George accepted a more lucrative appointment with the Northern Rhodesia Government and departed rather suddenly – much too quickly for his numerous creditors in Messina. The latter descended on George's few items of furniture and all that was left for one latecomer was the lion skin reposing in the tree. Later I saw the properly mounted skin in the creditor's shop and it was certainly a prize, the jaws wide open as if roaring a challenge almost as fierce as the price being asked by the new owner.

An American, visiting Messina Mine from the coast not long afterwards, snapped up the skin for £125 – and admitted that he would willingly have paid twice the asking price. And so it was that George, the dip supervisor, paid off one of his debts in all innocence and with very liberal interest.

CHAPTER FIFTEEN
Extended Patrol

Back at Gwanda District Headquarters, I was greeted with the sad news of the death of my little fox-terrier, Judy. Of course, I immediately recalled the peculiar vision of the dog I had experienced on the banks of the Limpopo at the precise hour of her tragic accident. A week or so later a fellow trooper returned with several bull terrier puppies – the mother had been torn to pieces by a troop of baboons. The one I picked came to my whistle – that of the Golden Oriole – within a very short time and I named him "Blanco". For many years he was to be my pal and constant companion, and to the best of my knowledge, he outlived all his brothers who were put up for adoption that day at the Gwanda police camp.

After I had completed the last entries on my patrol reports to the Limpopo and Mtetengwe areas, I was instructed on my next task. A trooper was being transferred to Fort Tuli on the Shashi and it was decided that four others, including myself, would take him down and, at the same time, conduct an extended patrol of all the West Nicholson and Gwanda areas before arriving at Tuli.

In charge of the patrol was Dan, a senior trooper from the West Nicholson police post. He was also the recipient of one of the bull terrier pups so Blanco was to have company – and the rest of us fun and games when we camped for the evening. A regularly-scheduled attraction was the tussle between the pups for Dan's cup after we had finished our evening cocoa. Blanco usually lost out in the struggle for the dregs and sugar at the bottom of Dan's cup but perhaps his heart wasn't in it because he knew full well that he'd be given my cup to lick clean once the opposition had retreated with the prize.

The object of an extended patrol was to show the flag in as many places as possible during the six weeks or two months decided upon, with the mercenary aspect of checking licences high on the list of priorities. Dogs, vehicles and the native tax were important sources of revenue and one of our jobs was to check on payments and persuade those in arrears to hie themselves off to Gwanda and square their accounts with the District Commissioner. It was not a practical proposition to arrest the offenders – they would very soon have become a burden, in every respect, on the patrol as we would have been forced to feed and guard these minor offenders. Perhaps surprisingly, this gentler arm of the law worked and, later on the patrol, I came across a number of Africans returning from Gwanda after paying their taxes.

We started on Number One Patrol Area, up to the Lumane Siding, where we detached a trooper to go on to the Glass Block Ranch and another to the Insiza River area while the three remaining tackled the vast Gwanda Reserve.

A night stop early in the patrol was at the local dip tank. The lonely supervisor allowed us to share his accommodation and was very glad of our company. We appreciated having a meal from a table instead of off the ground even though these were early days of our travels.

One big problem, almost wherever we went during the patrol, was a shortage of water and it was a real chore to satisfy the needs of our substantial remuda of horses, pack mules and donkeys. First a hole had to be dug in the river sand and the water extracted by means of a dish – or less frequently by bucket. Then each animal had to be satisfied to some extent. That first night we were far from liberal in our ministrations, promising the animals a larger ration in the morning before we struck camp.

Next morning there was a heavy overcast – not unusual in May but conditions which seldom promised rain, especially at this time of the year. There was certainly no reason to amend our programme of splitting up to visit the numerous kraals and then meeting up again at a water hole lower down the river. We set about watering the animals but progress seemed even slower than on the previous evening. My responsibilities were "Charcoal", the Gwanda DSP's horse, and "Ulster", a fairly new arrival at Gwanda which I had in fact known as a remount in Depot. The constable delegated to work with me had tied Ulster to one of the poles that fenced the water hole while we concentrated on quenching Charcoal's considerable thirst.

It was at this stage that a mob of cattle – scenting and frantic for water – burst bellowing from the surrounding bush. The other constables tried in vain to turn the herd and Ulster, seeing the cattle bearing down on him and being unaccustomed to such frights, reared in panic and dislodged the fence pole. He then bolted toward the open river bed, dragging the timber behind him.

At once I set off after the frightened horse although he'd soon realised he wouldn't get very far very fast anchored to a substantial pole and had halted, trembling, some distance away. But Ulster was upset and as I neared him he trotted off again and, in so doing, the pole struck a stone, upended and struck him on the rump. This was more than enough to set him off again at a gallop, interspersed with "double-barrelled" kicks at the log which were effective only in injuring the tendons and making the horse more frightened than ever. By the time I had managed to cut him off, he was limping badly and blood was flowing freely from both hind legs.

Back at camp I administered primitive first aid by soaking one of my puttees in paraffin from a hurricane lamp which stemmed the bleeding. Another puttee served as a protective bandage for the more seriously injured left leg while a liberal sprinkling of boracic powder and idioform was sufficient treatment for the other limb.

The incident did upset the day's programme. The constable was instructed to walk Ulster slowly to the evening rendezvous leaving me to patrol alone on Charcoal. Fortunately I managed quite well without an interpreter, covered my allotted area surprisingly quickly and reached the agreed spot on the river relatively early in the afternoon. There I found that Ulster had been watered and was nibbling quite comfortably on the green grass of the riverbank. I quickly placed Charcoal in the same happy position, sought out a comfortable site for our camp and, with the constable, set about collecting firewood.

The other two patrols came in later and by 4.30 p.m. we were settled comfortably having tea and a bit of food when we heard a distant roaring. The noise reminded me of the Basutoland rivers coming down in spate – but this was the Gwanda Reserve in May with no sign of storm clouds in the sky! I was too shy to voice my opinion of the unusual sound until one of the native sergeants spoke up. "Umfula wa dcwala," (the river is coming down in flood).

A few minutes before this confirmation of my unspoken fear, I had been discussing with Dan the desirability of getting Ulster to the veterinary surgeon at Gwanda as soon as possible and it had been agreed that at dawn the next day I should return with the animal. The impending tide suggested that I get Ulster safely across the river while there was still time. This I did, securing the injured animal on a long reim to a stout tree well removed from the riverbed.

Re-crossing the dry river where some of the animals were still being laboriously watered, I caught my first glimpse of the flood – the crest of a wave between six and nine feet in height and carrying with it great trees and lesser brushwood, all moving forward relentlessly with the slow-motion authority of a battleship going into action. I shouted to the constables to get the animals clear of the sand and lost no time in scrambling myself for the safety of our campsite before the wall of water swept past.

The show lost none of its fascination after the initial tidal wave. We sat and wagered on the height the water would reach on the trees on the opposite bank. Meanwhile the evening prematurely darkened as the flimsy clouds of the day took on an ominous character. At six o'clock the river was still in full flood, completely covering the former stretch of dry sand and more. Later we learned that between four and five inches of hail and rain had fallen in Gwanda the previous night. This freak storm had ended all our water supply problems in the Gwanda Reserve – but had brought other difficulties in its turbulent, debris-strewn wake.

Ignoring the rushing waters which we could certainly hear if not see, we settled down to our evening meal with the kind of patient philosophy so necessary among those living close to nature. Tomorrow would be soon enough to re-assess our patrolling schedule and my own plans for returning to Gwanda.

But the excitement was far from over. Without warning the sergeant in charge of the African police rushed into our midst to kick sand over our blazing camp fire. "Elephants" was his explanation as he scooped up handfuls of sand and earth and smothered the flames. Then we heard them – branches breaking as the thirsty herd drove towards the unexpected dry-season bath. Fortunately they changed direction at the last minute to plunge into the river down-stream. By then our animals had caught the scent of the intruders.

There was panic in the horse lines, an outburst of snorting and whinneying and every single animal broke its tether. For some peculiar reason the animals bolted not into the bush but into the flooded river – perhaps because across the river lay the quickest route back to the safety of Gwanda. Before the elephants had interrupted our meal, I had been yarning to my colleagues about the flooded rivers of Basutoland and how as a youngster I had enjoyed swimming in those dangerous waters. I should have been less boastful. Dan turned to me: "Nothing will stop those horses now and tomorrow they'll be in Gwanda and we'll have a long walk. Let's see you save the situation by bringing them back!"

Swimming in flooded rivers during daylight when one could see and perhaps avoid the debris being carried along was one thing – to do so at night was an entirely different proposition. I tried to explain the dangers to Dan and ended by saying that I would make the attempt if he insisted. He didn't but just then a pale moon broke through the cloud covering to reveal a much more settled river than indicated by the noise it was making. I decided to give it a go after arranging with Dan that he would flash his torch to give me my bearings when I yelled, if and when I emerged on the opposite bank. There was no time to be lost if I was to stand an even chance of catching the eleven horses, mules and pack donkeys. I stripped completely and lowered myself into the river. It was icy – not unreasonably since it had been fuelled largely by hail. Striking out for the opposite bank, I soon ran into branches and debris in midstream but rather then battle against them, I allowed myself to be swept downstream while expending as little energy as possible to inch towards the far bank. I collided with a fairly large tree and the branches pulled me down. Taking a deep breath I risked diving under the obstacle to allow the tree to pass over me. It worked and when I surfaced again I discovered that I was almost within reach of the bank. I grabbed a bush and was so frozen that it took me a while to realise that it was one of the *wag 'n bietjie* thorn variety. Sprawling for a few minutes on the sand to regain my breath and circulation, I then shouted across the river and saw Dan's answering torch some fifty or sixty yards upstream.

Taking another deep breath, I covered my eyes with one hand and another equally sensitive part of my body with the other and dived into the scrub and thornbush in a direction I hoped would bring me to the tracks of our fleeing livestock. The role of Rhodesia's first "streaker" held no great thrill and the moon which was playing hide-and-seek among the clouds was only sufficient to prevent me from crashing into the larger trees. I was making for a kraal which I had visited earlier in the day, there hoping to summon some assistance in rounding up the horses providing they hadn't bolted beyond the village.

The vegetation thinned away from the river and I made better progress. Stopping for a breather after some minutes of hard running, I heard the sound of hooves on hard ground off to one side. Redoubling my efforts, I ran parallel to the sounds and then spotted the unmistakable silhouette of one of our horses, "Steve", leading the others in a leisurely gallop across the countryside. I yelled his name for all I was worth. He stopped and pricked his ears in my direction and I gave thanks that he was so much more disciplined than the ill-fated Ulster. Following Steve's example, the other horses paused in their flight. It was obvious that they had recovered from their initial fright but they were still nervous. If I approached them alone they were more than likely to bolt again. Some assistance was most desirable.

There was cleared land ahead of me and the horses, across which I took a converging course towards but ahead of the animals. Within seconds I discovered that the horses – wiser than I – were following the watersleigh path leading to the village and once on this track I made excellent progress. Soon I was rousing the occupants of the kraal and seeking their assistance in rounding up our horses. However, before issuing specific instructions, I had to do something about my nakedness.

Light filtered through the doorway of a nearby hut and, opening the door, my eyes fell on an old sack on the mud floor – before my eyes met those of three or four teenage maidens who were reclining on mats beyond the small smoking paraffin lamp. Despite the lack of a lamp glass to steady the light, the flickering illumination must have been enough for the girls – sidling past me they rushed from the hut yelling blue murder! Apologies could come later.

I secured the sack around my waist and dashed from the hut just in time to cut off the first of the horses as it entered the village along the sleigh path. The girls had been more effective than my earlier efforts in rousing the other inhabitants and with remarkably little difficulty we shepherded the horses into a convenient cattle kraal. Once the animals were secured, I begged as many reims and ropes as were available and was soon leading Steve and two of his companions back to the river. A couple of men from the village brought up the rear with the remaining animals who by now were completely manageable and all too innocent of the trouble they had caused me.

At the river bank I shouted news of my success to Dan before tying the animals securely to the trees – there was no point in trying to get the horses back across the river. Having checked the tethers to ensure there would be no further bids to escape to Gwanda, I went upstream and swam across to where I had left my clothes. Back in camp, Dan made me swallow two aspirins, two quinine tablets and a very stiff hot brandy. As a result I slept soundly until eight o'clock the following morning.

It was only then that I discovered that I was a mass of scratches from head to foot and it took another hour to extract all the *wag 'n bietjie* thorns from my body. By mid-morning the flood had subsided and after crossing the river I enjoyed the revenge of hanging onto the tail of several of the horses and allowing them to tow me over to our camp. This time I wore a pair of shorts.

With all the animals across, I made plans to leave for Gwanda on Charcoal and leading Ulster – who seemed no worse for his adventurous night. I wish I could have said the same. At district headquarters I handed the injured horse over for medical treatment and put in a full report on the incident. I was given a few days to collect supplies and then set off on Charcoal and leading a pack animal to rejoin the patrol.

I found them as the sun was setting and, what with the duiker they had shot and the tinned fruit, jam and other groceries I had brought, we celebrated our reunion in appropriate fashion. I had missed little – it was the first good meal the others had eaten since leaving the Gwanda Reserve.

CHAPTER SIXTEEN
Sick Interlude

The sudden flood described in my last chapter was not the only dampener on our scheduled extended patrol from Gwanda. We had to get the relieving detail to Tuli by a specified date but were still a far cry from completing our patrol task when Dan, who was in charge of the four-man expedition, went down with a bad attack of dysentery. We reviewed our plans and re-entered the Gwanda Reserve to take a more direct route to Tuli. Dan's condition worsened – he preferred to walk holding my stirrup than ride himself – and in the end it was decided to send the one trooper onto Tuli by himself, that I should escort Dan to Gwanda for medical treatment and that the fourth member of the patrol would do his best to complete the patrol assignment with the constables, the camp followers and all the equipment.

Dan and I made slow progress until we reached the edge of the reserve where there was a general dealer's store. Among the medical comforts of the proprietor was a bottle of port – the well-known if medically unsubstantiated cure for stomach disorders. Half a glass of the wine, mixed with the same quantity of goat's milk which we obtained from a local tribesman, significantly reduced Dan's griping pains and checked his dysentery. He regained some strength and we made Gwanda the following day.

There was no criticism of my second unscheduled return to DHQ but a few days later I too went sick with a violent headache which nothing would relieve. I took myself off to Gwanda Hospital where I was put to bed. The splitting headache returned each time I raised my head from the pillow to take the medicine prescribed by the doctor.

On the third day the glands in my crotch swelled and it was then that the doctor discovered a hard-backed bont tick with its head buried in my flesh. He carefully removed the intruder and within 24 hours my temperature was down and the headache disappeared. It took me some time to recover from the attack of tick-bite fever but it made me realise the agonies suffered by dogs and cattle in similar straits. All I wanted was to be left in peace to die.

One morning during the later part of my convalescence I was passing the doctor's house where I found him in his pyjamas conversing in the most endearing tones with four fluffy kittens. What was less understandable was that he was pushing each kitten in turn through a small hole in the gauze around his sleeping porch but grabbing the tail of each animal and pulling it back before it made its escape. I asked him what on earth he was doing. His reply was that he was "cleaning up their coats!" I'm afraid I didn't agree with his morning grooming procedure – it was obvious the kittens didn't either.

One thing I had learned from that first extended patrol were the respective merits of wearing khaki shorts as opposed to issue riding breeches during those long days on horseback. It had been Dan who had advised me that shorts were more comfortable but I had cursed him thoroughly at the end of the first day after my knees had been terribly sunburnt. A cooling shower of rain had at first been welcomed – until the water blisters made their appearance. It was only after applying lead and opium, used for our animals' sore backs, that I was able to sleep. Had I worn breeches, I'm sure the tick would never have wormed its way up my legs and I would have been spared those splitting headaches.

When I recovered and returned to duty I was pleased to find that my servant had been looking after my bull terrier, Blanco, feeding him daily and keeping him relatively free of ticks. The pup was about to have company.

I was cleaning my equipment one afternoon when the constable on grazing guard duty brought me a newly born blue-faced monkey which he had found abandoned in the veld where the horses were grazing. I rewarded him for saving the infant from certain death and then set my mind to the problem of feeding the orphan. He was too young to lap milk. Finally I hit upon the idea of using my fountain pen's rubber ink reservoir as a teat. It worked well – both for feeding the baby and as a comforter when he woke up in the early hours crying for his mother.

The monkey thrived and he and Blanco became the best of friends. He would leap on the dog's back, grab his collar and ride around the camp. Poor old Blanco took it all good-naturedly, despite the fact that the monkey often used the dog's tail to hoist himself on to his "mount".

On my next patrol I was obliged to take my family with me. The monkey came along in Charcoal's nosebag, with his head poking out of the top, while Blanco accompanied his second master, my private servant, bringing up the rear with the mule. This was to be another wet patrol.

One evening, the storm clouds gathered and although I had my patrol tent on the pack mule, no such luxuries were provided for the constable or my servant. I decided to make for the nearest village where the kraalhead was sympathetically disposed towards the police. If the storm did break, there would be some protection for my companions in the village.

It was dark when we reached the kraal and, while the storm was still threatening, we had to hurry to erect my tent by torchlight and then get the saddlery and equipment under its cover. I had just laid out my bed for the night when the skies opened. The others ran for the huts and although the old headman had offered me similar accommodation, I opted for the tent where all my belongings were. As a precaution, however, I put on my greatcoat and with the issue trenching tool, banked up the soil at the higher end of the tent to divert any flow of water.

In the darkness I had failed to see that the tent had been pitched in a depression and no sooner had I re-entered the tent to take cover than I realised my mistake. But it was too late to make amends. My shouts for help to the constable were drowned by thunder and the sheets of rain. Suddenly a wall of water hit my modest dam, spilled over and flooded under the tent. I charged out with the torch and trenching tool but my best efforts were completely in vain.

Steeling myself for a most unpleasant night, I went back into the tent to find Blanco and the monkey virtually afloat on a pillow while the blankets on the groundsheet heaved up and down as the water rippled beneath the groundsheet. All the equipment was soaked. My one thought was to get my pets to safety so I gathered them up and braved the storm to take them to my servant.

I was completely drenched when I returned to the tent. By this time a small river was running between the poles. My blankets had already been swept away in a sodden mess and a change of clothing which I normally carried in the blanket roll was also gone. All I could do was sit mournfully on one of the grocery boxes and wait for the deluge to stop.

Eventually the downpour ceased and I was able to light the hurricane lamp. One of the few relatively dry pieces of equipment was the mule's pack saddle which had been placed over the bag containing the animals' rations of crushed mealies. By turning the pack saddle over on its metal arches, I had at least a seat above the sodden ground. With a careful arrangement of my own saddle and the grocery boxes, I was able to make a bed of sorts. Taking off my soaked boots and leggings, I eventually fell asleep with the lantern providing warmth and something of a steam bath.

I was up at dawn next morning to recover my washed away clothing which had been taken by the flood. By the time everything was more or less dry, it was midday. We moved off, hardly refreshed by the wet night. Late in the afternoon I reached the Mtsabezi Mission where the children immediately fell in love with my monkey and begged me to give it to them. I made sure their father agreed and then parted with my little pet, although by this time he was lapping up milk and porridge as fast as it was given to him. I visited him a month later when he had grown up out of all recognition. He had obviously been given a good home. I wondered if that one wet night was as deeply engraved on his memory as it was on mine. I learned another lesson – never attempt to pitch camp in darkness.

CHAPTER SEVENTEEN
Fort Rixon

After a few more patrols in the Gwanda District, I was told of my transfer to Fort Rixon, a post which controlled an area consisting mainly of white farms and which promised a change from roughing it in the reserves. I rode Charcoal to my new station with a pack animal in tow with most of my equipment. An overnight stop at Filabusi gave the troopers there every opportunity of telling me all about my new post and the neighbouring Shangani area.

It all sounded very exciting and I was on my way at sunrise, reaching my destination that evening.

Fort Rixon camp was at the foot of a kopje – most convenient in that target-shooting butts had been built into the hillside only a stone's throw from the station. There was a cleared square in front of the barrack rooms and offices and there was even a tennis court for those off-duty hours. On the other side of the parade ground were the stables and horse lines, the constables' quarters and the modest cell block. The Union Jack fluttered over the square – as if it was necessary to remind visitors that this was indeed an outpost of the British Empire.

The tennis court was more than a scenic decoration. The locals had formed a tennis club and on Saturday afternoons the young and the old took it in turns to exercise. Competitions were arranged on a regular basis and these brought in workers and their wives from the surrounding mines (mostly small-workings) and farms. The club served the dual purpose of business and pleasure as the local policemen were able to meet their public and discuss with them the problems that cropped up from time to time.

With so many white residents in the area it was perhaps strange that the first case I should be called upon to investigate concerned the attempted murder of an African by a local headman, Mjegeni, who lived some twenty miles from the camp on the boundary of the enormous De Beers ranch. The circumstances were that a beerdrink had been in progress at a particular kraal when the headman arrived, bringing with him his cherished status symbol, a shot-gun. One of the locals, not a Matabele, challenged the headman who was actually of Khumalo Royal blood and the latter took umbrage and decided to teach the mere Msutu a lesson – by stabbing him with a knife. This wound, as we later discovered, penetrated to the extent of touching the victim's left lung. But not content with the knife assault, the headman loaded his shotgun and discharged it over the prostrate body of his victim. The affair disrupted the beerdrink, not unnaturally, and the headman returned home.

By the time I reached the scene the next day the victim was in a bad state. He had bled profusely from his wound and was too weak to walk. I arranged for a sleigh to be harnessed to four oxen, provided bedding of thatching grass and treated the wound to the best of my ability before setting off on the slow journey back to Fort Rixon. The Msutu's wife and another man came along to ensure that the casualty stayed on the primitive ambulance and we arrived at the camp without incident. There my temporary dressing was removed, further treatment was given and the patient then sent to hospital in Bulawayo.

The victim made a rapid recovery and was quite fit for the High Court hearing which came some six weeks later. I thought I would be required to give no more than formal evidence of arrest but I was mistaken.

During the proceedings the police court official came across the original statement I had taken down in writing after having duly warned and cautioned the accused. When I took the stand to give evidence of arrest, he passed this statement to me and asked me to read it. I received a measure of censure from the judge because this important document had not been produced at the preliminary hearing in the subordinate court at Fort Rixon. I explained that the evidence I had given then was a synopsis of the facts contained in the statement I was now holding. The learned judge disagreed with the accuracy of my "synopsis" but after argument between defending and prosecuting counsel, it was finally agreed that my original statement – which amounted to an admission of guilt – should be entered on the court record. The final question from the judge was whether I was fluent in the Sindebele language to which I was able to answer in the affirmative.

Somewhat thankfully after this unexpected grilling, I returned to my seat relieved that I had escaped the witness stand before the judge thought up some more embarrassing questions for a basically district policeman. The headman was then asked if he wished to call witnesses – which he didn't – and then volunteered to give his own account of what had taken place.

He related that after arriving at the scene of the beerdrink, he had entered one of the huts where some women were sitting around a fire. One of them was the complainant's wife, and the accused had taken a seat on the opposite side of the fire from her. Before anything untoward took place, the complainant himself entered the hut, picked up a stool carved from a single log of wood and, beating time with this very substantial gavel, asked the accused why he was always trying to make advances to his wife. The prosecution asked what reply the headman had made to this allegation and his answer in the vernacular reduced the official interpreter to a fit of suppressed laughter. Meanwhile the Bench and the non-linguists in the court waited expectantly for a translation. With a great deal of self-control, helped by the knowledge that this was the High Court of Rhodesia and that a man was on trial for attempted murder and trying hard to keep a straight face, the interpreter whispered to the judge that the accused's reply had been another question – did the complainant think that he (the headman) was as physically endowed as a donkey that he could reach the man's wife on the other side of the fire?

His Honour and the two assessors – as one man – fished handkerchiefs from their robes and covered their mouths. After an interval the judge announced that the court would adjourn for fifteen minutes. What took place behind the closed doors of the judge's chambers did not appear on the court record although little imagination is needed to guess what transpired.

When the court re-assembled the accused continued to give evidence on his own behalf. The outcome was that the victim's allegation of adultery was considered insufficient provocation for the headman's assault with the knife. Furthermore, as a headman he had fired his shotgun quite unnecessarily in the presence of a large number of villagers who might have been seriously hurt. In his position he should have known better and he deserved the sentence of eighteen months' hard labour.

My first appearance in the High Court, despite the lighter moments of the case, was an experience I was not anxious to repeat. For the rest of my service – by dint of much wheeling

and dealing – I made sure I steered clear of the paraded majesty
of the law in High Court Session.

CHAPTER EIGHTEEN
Motorbikes and Warlords

A young clerk in the Fort Rixon Native Department succumbed to the temptation of buying a motor-cycle on the hire-purchase scheme (such traps for the unwary were in existence even in those days!) After a couple of months, however, he drove up to the police camp and asked if I would accept his machine and the financial liability of keeping up the monthly payments. I felt sorry for him – he had been crippled with poliomyelitis in childhood – and in spite of some reservations I agreed to sign the necessary papers transferring the motorcycle and its financial responsibilities to me.

The acquisition of the motorcycle proved most useful for the speedy investigation of cases of housebreaking and theft, sudden deaths and, in some cases, stock theft. I was able to get to the scene much quicker than by horse and pack mule. With a carrier on the back of the machine, I was able to take the native constable too.

But there were disadvantages. There was a time when faction fights between Matabeles and Mashonas broke out in Bulawayo and an urgent telegram summoned all policemen with motor-cycles from the districts. I was told to report to the Bulawayo Camp where I was instructed to act as despatch rider.

A different assignment came one afternoon when it was reported that an African armed with a muzzle-loader and an assegai had been seen crossing Dr Vigne's property on the Khami Road. I went to investigate. Having parked the motorcycle, I walked up the garden path to the gauzed door, knocked, identified myself and asked for Dr Vigne.

"Dr Vigne is out," replied a voice from within.

I knocked again, repeated my request and received the same answer. I asked for Mrs Vigne – to be told: "Dr Vigne is out!"

Frustrated, I asked the speaker to come out and was again met with "Dr Vigne is out". I began to wonder if the person within the house was deaf or merely queer in the head and, exasperated, I explained the purpose of my visit. Again I was told "Dr Vigne is out", an announcement which was followed by a shrill whistle and the more threatening, "See him off, Brutus!"

I gave up and was halfway to my motorcycle when, laughing their heads off, Mrs Vigne and her daughter rushed out of the house.

"It was only old Polly playing his usual tricks," they explained. I was invited in and entertained with Polly's version of "Show me the way to go home". Over a cup of tea I saw the funny side of the prank but, getting down to business, was unable to verify the report of the armed African. Miss Vigne was being courted by a young policeman, whose health was enquired after with tender solicitude, and I began to suspect that the report had been made in hopes of securing the attendance of another and more special policeman.

It was while I was in Bulawayo on these special duties that I first came face-to-face with a most eccentric officer known as "The Warlord". We met when I was on night duty and he walked into the office. I immediately stood to attention and answered smartly when he asked my name and age. Then he turned the lamp shade, so that I was bathed in the full glare – in best interrogation style, adjusted his monocle and announced "I was soldiering before you were born!" It was almost as if he was tempting me to argue with him. He then dialed the Civil Commissioner's number and reported "All quiet on the location front" in the most dramatic tones.

I had heard many stories about the Warlord and this first sight of the man gave me no cause to doubt the truth of most of them. One such tale had been told to me – first hand as it were – by the farrier who had visited Fort Rixon and had been reluctant, to say the least, to shoe my one-eyed pack horse, Maggie.

It transpired that the farrier had arrived at another station which included Maggie on strength although she had just been boarded because of her eye injury, on the same day that the Warlord was carrying out an inspection. His nickname had been earned because of his fanaticism for military manoeuvres which he insisted should be practised as frequently and as realistically as possible.

The farrier-corporal's hopes that the inspection would not involve him were short-lived. The Warlord ordered him to saddle Maggie and parade with the rest of the station personnel – even the camp sergeant-major had to appear on the square with full equipment. The men and their mounts were lined up before the officer with Maggie on the right flank. On the command "Prepare to Mount", Maggie gave a snort. The word "Mount" was too much for the half-blinded horse. With one terrific leap she sent the unfortunate farrier-corporal over her arched neck. A second leap sent her over the prostrate form of her would-be rider who had entwined the reins around his left wrist. Thereafter Maggie tore around the parade ground – which had been scoffled of weeds and grass in honour of the Warlord's visit and consisted only of sand, gravel and dust – with the poor farrier firmly in tow. After two or three circuits the reins mercifully parted and Maggie, relieved of her burden, trotted back to the stables still snorting with fright.

The farrier picked himself up – covered in dust and minus every brass button from his tunic – and waited for the Warlord's volley. It wasn't quite what he expected.

"Now that, men, is what I call sheer guts. This man – with howitzers booming, machine guns rattling and trench mortars landing on target – still hangs on to his horse." He turned to the farrier: "Well done, Corporal. You've had your baptism of fire – and you may now file away to the casualty tent for treatment."

Perhaps the farrier was not that unfortunate. The Warlord put the rest of the parade through every exercise in the cavalryman's book and a few more. They were ordered to dismount and charge up a kopje. Then, having silenced an imaginary machine-gun nest, they were ordered back to their horses to charge, in line abreast, a donga which contained imaginary trench mortars. By the time they had scaled every kopje with rifles and fixed bayonets and charged every threatening donga in the neighbourhood, not only the men but also their horses were bathed in perspiration. The Warlord reassembled his panting troops on the parade ground, sheathed his sword which that day had cut down dozens of the imaginary enemy, and announced that he was not at all satisfied with the performance. The exercise would be repeated the following day ... "when I trust there will be a little more action!"

The troopers thought hard that evening and the farrier-corporal needed little persuasion to announce the next morning that all the horses were unfit for duty. It was not far from the truth, anyway. The Warlord took the news calmly.

"Is that so? Well, I suppose yesterday's exercise was rather strenuous. Very good, Corporal – file away and attend to your horses."

The officer then turned to the sergeant-major and announced his intention of inspecting the stores. There the Warlord found a pile of broom handles.

"Ah!" he breathed in satisfaction. "Just what I was looking for. Take these to the barracks and tell each man to attach his bridle to the broomstick of his choice and assemble on the parade ground in thirty minutes. The horses may be knocked up but we can still carry out the troop drills."

Sure enough, the troopers and the sergeant-major paraded with their hobby-horses at the required time. But when the Warlord gave the order to mount, all hell broke loose. Broomsticks started to buck, helmets were dislodged and one rider after another disappeared into the surrounding bush, valiantly trying to control his mount.

"What the devil's happening, Sergeant-Major?" roared the Warlord.

"Sorry, Sir ... I can't hold him ..." replied the sergeant-major as his bucking broomstick took him in the wake of his departing troops. The Warlord turned away in utter disgust.

Later that evening the troops returned, leading their broomsticks and making much of their imaginary horses which by now had all been named. Then having removed the bridles, they watered their mounts before returning them to the storeroom-stable.

The episode put an end to the officer's full-dress military manoeuvres. He was transferred to Bulawayo which is where I met him and confirmed for myself that the Warlord was a most peculiar character.

CHAPTER NINETEEN
Exercise and Expertise

Life at Fort Rixon had its quieter moments and my favourite recreation was to saddle Charcoal and, with Blanco at the horse's heels, take an exercise ride along one of the nearby valleys. I owned a genuine English-made exercise saddle, a beautiful snaffle bit and reins and Charcoal looked every bit the three-quarter-bred Arab he was when saddled. He was officially recorded as a brown gelding but next to Blanco – especially if the dog had been bathed the night before – Charcoal's name showed his true colour!

One Sunday morning the three of us were taking the morning air a mile or so from the camp when Charcoal pricked up his ears and started prancing. I turned my head from a general appreciation of a lovely day and there, less than two hundred yards ahead, was a large cock ostrich. It was too good an opportunity for some excitement. Leaning forward over Charcoal's neck I hissed "Saaa ..." It was enough. Like an arrow my mount leapt into full gallop and as we took off I glanced back to see poor old Blanco straining every muscle to keep up. His hind legs seemed to touch his ears and the sides of his mouth were strained in the grin of the typical "Bonzo" character.

The ground was soft after a light shower the previous night and Charcoal was churning up clods of black earth which did nothing to help Blanco's vision or speed. Meanwhile, the ostrich was treating the chase more seriously, swaying and flapping his wings as his panic increased.

We closed on the now-frantic bird and then our quarry swerved suddenly to the right. A second later I hurriedly revised my opinion on the bird's change of direction as an enormous antbear hole appeared in our path. Charcoal was up to the challenge. He cocked his ears, judged his take-off perfectly and cleared the hole and a mound beyond with yards to spare.

Blanco was much less successful. Because of the flying earth he'd had no warning of the obstacle and by the time I had recovered from the jump enough to look back, he was in the process of somersaulting straight into the hole. The acrobatics upset Blanco's sense of direction. With scarcely a pause he was up and running again – but in the direction we had just come from! When I yelled to him, the look of surprise on his face was so amusing that I couldn't help roaring with laughter. I was still chuckling after I'd dismounted and the three of us were resting under a mimosa – Blanco's tongue was hanging out a good ten inches as he slobbered his apologies for being such a fool.

Amusing but in a much more serious vein was the experience I had soon after the ostrich-hunting incident. No. 2 area's regular trooper was away in Bulawayo and I was detailed to investigate the alleged theft of a bunch of keys. The complainant was a retired army major trying his hand at ranching, who had reported the theft of his storeroom keys while he'd been issuing his employees with their rations. There was a measure of seriousness and urgency about the case beyond the mere insecurity of a storeroom, the padlock of which could be replaced. On the same keyring was the major's safe key and the safe contained the month's payroll.

It took all day for me to reach the ranch with two constables and it was almost sunset when I reported to the major. He'd spent his time since reporting the theft dreaming up the best means of investigation and was convinced that the culprit was a tenant, Mbothela, who had – in parlance – previous convictions.

I was left in little doubt that I should immediately send one of the constables to arrest the suspect, search his hut and return with both accused and missing keys. It was not possible, I argued. Both constables had walked all day to reach the ranch and it would be dark by the time one of them reached the suspect's hut, some six miles away, and a thorough search would be impossible. To give him his due, the major accepted my reasoning and offered me a meal and his spare room for the night. Again I declined, wanting to attend to the horses and too tired myself for the social graces.

We saw to the needs of the horses, Maggie and Charcoal, and then erected my tent near the insecure storeroom beside which was a pile of discarded farm equipment. Over supper – a modest meal of bully beef and biscuits – and several cups of tea, I thought over the case of the missing keys. The major had described the very substantial keyring, complete with chain and leather buttonhole, something which could hardly have been palmed with ease. Despite all the hubbub of issuing rations, it was unlikely that someone, such as the suspect who had no valid reason to be present, would go unnoticed. The major had grudgingly admitted that Mbothela had not been seen near the homestead at the time of the disappearance of the keys. But before getting my head down, I carefully instructed one of the constables to be off at the crack of dawn to search the suspect's hut – not overlooking the thatching – and advise him that he was "helping the police with their enquiries".

After a restful night I was up and shaved long before the major made his appearance. He repeated his suspicions regarding Mbothela, showed me exactly where the padlock and keys had been and made sure that I shared his worries about the payroll in the safe. I listened politely, reserving my own opinion until the arrival of the suspect and his escort.

The pair made good time and by mid-morning I was questioning the old Matabele from my seat among the discarded ploughs. Mbothela was polite and helpful – if not in the way the major had expected. I was frank with him.

"You know that everyone here knows that you have been in jail?"

"Yes, N'kosi," he admitted, "but I am not the only thief that lives here." He carried his head high and proudly held my gaze as I watched for signs of discomfort. All that I was able to detect was a moistness in his eyes.

"Who are the others in this place who are thieves?"

"The boss-boy, Hendrik, he is also a thief."

"What have you seen him steal?"

"A big fat *inhayi* belonging to the owner of this farm."

"When was this sheep stolen?"

"A few days ago."

"Where were you when this happened?"

"I was visiting the compound."

"Did you see the sheep being killed?"

"No, N'kosi, it was killed in the veld and the meat brought to the compound during the night."

The questioning went on and on and slowly but surely I established the facts surrounding not the theft of the keys but the slaughter of an apparently valuable sheep. Before becoming a tenant, Mbothela had worked on the ranch and was familiar with the major's livestock. Unfairly coining a phrase that it takes a thief to catch a thief, Mbothela had noticed that a particularly large animal, distinctively black and white, was missing from the flock which he saw on his way home after visiting the compound. He told me where the sheep were usually grazed, in a field near some wild figs I had passed on my way to the ranch

I jotted down all this information, overlooking the matter of the keys for the time being, and then told the old Matabele to wait with the constables. I was already mounted on Charcoal when the major arrived and wanted to know where I was going. I passed on the information gleaned from Mbothela and was mildly surprised that the major relied solely on his boss-boy and his herd-boy to tell him if and when any of the sheep was missing. But of course they were much more reliable than the old jailbird who was merely leading me up the garden path!

The major had told me that his sheep had been moved to another paddock, but without difficulty I found the place Mbothela had described, including the fig trees under which I sat as I pondered my next move. I tried to reconstruct the crime – if indeed one had been committed. The paddock was huge and to begin with I didn't know what I was looking for or where to look for it. Slowly I thought it all out. Just as I'd scrambled for the shade of the fig trees, so would the sheep. Proof of my reasoning was the dung – some of it quite fresh – scattered around me.

A slight breeze rustled the leaves of the trees and Blanco raised his nose which he'd been trying to cool on a shady outcrop. I followed his gaze and noticed the freshly-cut stump of a branch. Examining it more closely, I discovered that it was unmistakably mutton fat. Glancing down, I saw that there were spots of what could only be congealed blood on some of the fallen leaves. I started gathering them until I realised that they were poor evidence for a charge of stock theft.

Blanco came to my rescue again. He was digging earnestly in the shallow earth that covered this type of rocky terrain. I went across to help him with his excavations and after a few minutes of digging with a dry stick, I felt something soft and alien in the ground. Using the branch as a hook, I unearthed firstly the leg of a sheepskin and then the rest of the evidence. Mbothela had not lied. Here was the skin of a very large black and white sheep.

After this discovery, more evidence came readily to hand. There were chips of bone amid the leaves, indicating that the carcass had been hastily butchered; there was a charred rib bone which I rescued from Blanco and which later turned out to have been a bribe to the herd-boy to say nothing of the slaughter in return for a few hastily grilled mutton chops.

Charcoal wasn't very happy about my concealing the sheepskin beneath the saddle blanket for the return to the homestead but I didn't want to give the game away too soon. I off-saddled at the major's veranda, dumping saddle, blanket and sheepskin at his feet and he wasn't too happy either. He thawed considerably when I told him the result of my investigations and raised no objections when I said I was going to arrest his boss-boy and his shepherd. He offered me a drink which I accepted gratefully.

I had almost forgotten about the missing keys as I returned to my seat amid the abandoned farm machinery. While marshalling the facts concerning the dead sheep, my eyes fell on a bleached stalk of grass protruding from beneath a discarded plough disc. Someone had recently disturbed the junk and I felt I would have noticed the significance of the bleached stalk earlier while sitting in the same position interrogating Mbothela. Who had been nosing around my camp site while I'd been out at the paddock?

With my riding crop I lifted the plough disc. There was the major's bunch of keys.

I left the keys exactly where they were lying, walked over to the homestead and summoned the major. Perhaps I showed off a little in escorting him to the junk heap, asking him if he noticed anything peculiar about a particular plough disc and then inviting him to raise it and find the keys for himself. But I'd reckoned he'd earned some humility for jumping to conclusions about Mbothela while throwing cold water on my suspicions about his "so reliable" boss-boy.

The uncovery – in more ways than one – of both the theft of the sheep and the theft of the keys cemented our friendship. The major warmly invited me to dinner, before which I telephoned the sergeant at Fort Rixon while trying hard to keep the elation out of my report. Unknowingly I'd qualified for my next job – a nearby farmer had reported the loss of no less than twenty-four Blackheaded Persian sheep.

Who had stolen the keys and then put them under the plough disc I never discovered, although I had my suspicions about Hendrik. Honour was satisfied when I sent him and the shepherd, several witnesses who were prepared to give evidence and the exhibits themselves back to Fort Rixon the next day, all safely escorted by one of the constables. With them went Mbothela – who had turned out to be not such a black sheep after all.

To me was left the task of finding two dozen very distinctive black sheep.

CHAPTER TWENTY
Ostrich of Trouble

Before telling of the second sheep-stealing case which followed directly upon my unveiling of the army major's "faithful retainer" with a predilection for roast mutton – and my Sherlock Holmes-type solution to the mystery of the missing keys – let me digress again "for the birds" and devote more to the subject of ostriches.

It will be recalled that I had been sent to look into the second sheep-stealing – of two dozen Blackheaded Persians – at Cock's Farm, at the time I had only just put an end to the army major's troubles. There was no need for me to return to Fort Rixon and I was on my way to investigate the second case at first light on the morning of finding *both* keys to the earlier mystery.

It was a glorious day – the freshness of the morning, the smell of the sweet grass and the bird songs which filled the air made it wonderful to be alive. I was well ahead of my pack team and my solitary joy translated itself into traditional Irish melodies of my boy-hood as a prelude to equally foreign hill-billy ballads which were much more in harmony with Charcoal's rolling gait than the questionably Gaelic lilt. The surrounding country was devoid of trees and its monotony in this respect made it all the more understandable that the local gentry – particularly the younger and less gentlemanly types – adapted the excitement of fox-hunting in their own inimitable style.

The "fox" was almost invariably a wily, never-snared bird – a cock ostrich known as "Steve"; the huntsmen's mount was a half-ton truck and the ever-hopeful means of contact was a lassoo.

From all reports, Steve enjoyed the hunt as much as his pursuers. His favourite method of evasion at the moment of crisis was to swing his neck one way while body and legs charged off in an entirely different direction – a defence which I suppose only a giraffe could hope to emulate. But it wasn't that easy to reach the point at which the hunter cast his lot – or rather, his lassoo – because Steve had an inbuilt knowledge of every anthole in the area and more often than not it was a question of ostrich versus machine: the hunters battling with their truck as well as the more obvious prey. Broken springs, buckled wheels and bent axles not to mention broken bones and bruises sustained as the would-be hunters were suddenly thrown from their insecure perches on the back of the truck, were typical results of a day's hunting!

Wisely, perhaps, I had resisted the temptation to join in the fun, but I did have a memorable confrontation with a cock ostrich which might have been Steve when a colleague and I were on our way back to Fort Rixon having fired the annual musketry course at Filabusi.

Steve and his kin were a particular nuisance for their disrespect for farm fences. Trooper Wallace and I were returning from Filabusi when we decided to make a social call on a certain farmer. That it was lunchtime when we passed the farm also had something to do with our "showing the flag". The owner of this property had complained long and loud about a cock ostrich which was breaking down his fences as fast as he repaired them and in desperation had offered a reward of £5 to anyone able to put a finish to his troubles. But the ostrich, thus far, had been far too cunning.

We actually encountered the owner and his manager on the stoep of the farmhouse as we rode up. They were looking mournfully towards a distant line of trees beside a small stream. As we reined in and greeted the pair, our welcome was interrupted by an oath.

"My God! There's the old swine back again. Damned if he hasn't burst through that paddock where the cows are!"

Wallace and I followed his gaze and there, in a clearing amid the mimosa trees, was a magnificent ostrich – "cocky" in every respect. The farmer turned to us and, addressing my half-section, asked if we had seen a youngster from a neighbouring farm tearing about the countryside on a motorcycle. Indeed, we had heard the machine – as a biking enthusiast, it hadn't escaped my attention – but we were both a little mystified at the connection between the motorcycle and the ostrich. An explanation was quickly forthcoming: "Young Bobby has been here every day for the past week, trying to earn the 'Dead or Alive' reward of £5, but the ostrich seems to know only too well what Bobby's after. He lays low whenever he hears the motorbike and then flaunts himself with all the cheek in the world when Bobby has gone. It's damned insulting, that's what it is!"

The owner – as opposed to his farm manager – was a Cockney reputed to have earned a small fortune on the London Stock Exchange. Although his farming knowledge was very limited, he was highly respected in the neighbourhood for his quiet manner and his deep interest in cattle – particularly his ambition of breeding up a high quality herd of which he could be proud one day.

He had paddocked his farm at considerable expense for proper control over his small herd and the fence-breaking ostrich was frustrating all his carefully-laid out plans. His quiet nature and his love of animals had boiled over into encouraging the early demise of the marauder. As policemen, Wallace and I could perhaps be of assistance and have some fun at the same time.

"Would you like us to have a go at him or are you reserving him for Bobby?" I enquired.

"Reserving him be damned!" retorted the normally mild-mannered farmer. "If either of you two chaps can shoot the old bastard, I'll pay you the reward and give you a free lunch into the bargain."

Wallace and I were only too keen to have a go.

"Right, Pam," said my half-section. "Let's toss for it."

I readily agreed – and won the toss.

As I picked up my rifle, I wondered if winning the toss had really been such good fortune. After annual musketry my rifle was in sparkling condition. Was it worth all the trouble of boiling out the barrel, endlessly pulling it through and so on, just for the one or two shots necessary to despatch the ostrich.

With these mixed feelings I loaded the magazine and walked towards the trees where my prey was still clearly visible. Using the scant mimosa as cover, I was within a few hundred yards of the ostrich when he bestirred himself into a gentle trot across my front. Breaking cover I threw a round into the breech, the noise had the expected effect on my intended victim. He increased speed and swerved. I aimed about a yard in front of the base of his long neck and squeezed the trigger, almost reconciled to a miss on the small fastmoving target as I fired. But to my amazement, the ostrich crumbled in mid-stride and dropped motionless. I reloaded and waited for what must have been a full minute. A slight breeze floated down the paddock, barely fluttering the feathers of the downed bird. I closed in and gasped at my good luck. The single shot had broken the troublesome cock's neck – by far the most difficult part of the grotesquely proportioned bird to hit.

Unloading the rifle, I sauntered proudly back to the stoep where the clatter of plates indicated that lunch was already underway inside the dining room.

"Hard luck, Palmer," sympathised our host. "As soon as we saw the scoundrel break into a run, we knew you had no choice. Never mind, sit down and have some lunch."

"Didn't you hear the shot?" I parried.

"Oh, yes, we heard it all right. In fact we were surprised that you even bothered to waste your ammunition."

"It wasn't wasted," I retorted quietly.

"What do you mean?"

"That cock ostrich will bother you no more. He's as dead as a doornail."

"Go on!" exclaimed the owner. "You're pulling my leg."

"I'm not, sir," I protested. "Go and see for yourself."

Getting up from his seat at the head of the table, he walked out on to the veranda where he had left the binoculars. I could see that he was still far from convinced.

"Cor blimey!" he gasped, reverting to his native accent. "You actually got him. Hey, George," he called to the manager. "Come and see. The old bastard's dead." He handed the binoculars to his employee. "Hang on to these while I go down and make sure."

"There's no need for that – what about your soup which is getting cold?" I reminded him. "Let's have lunch and then take a look."

"Not on your life," came the response. However my host did delegate his responsibilities. "George, go down there right away with the shotgun and make sure that damned bird is not shamming." Again I argued that it was a waste of time. I'd already made sure the ostrich wasn't playing possum.

As soon as George returned to confirm the kill, the owner took out his cheque book. I asked that instead of giving me the reward – I'd really done no more than my duty as a policeman – he make a donation to charity. This action was also appropriate, I thought, because the ostrich menace had been ended by such a fortunate shot which I explained in detail as we concluded the meal. By no stretch of the imagination could I claim that marksmanship rather than a one-in-a-thousand fluke shot had been responsible and I felt no sense of being robbed of reputation when our host spread the story around the district, the punch line being: "I don't know who was more surprised – Palmer or the ostrich!"

This episode, in itself clearly recalled over half-a-century's adventures, merges with forgotten dates and details to the extent that I'm unable to remember if the ostrich I killed was the notorious Steve. I've recounted the incident here because as I rode along the track beside a fenced paddock on my way to Cock's Farm to answer my successive complaint of sheep-stealing, I noticed here and there evidence of repair work to the fence. At the same time, my horse Charcoal became unaccountably agitated and looking around carefully, I spied the heads of perhaps half-a-dozen ostrich. As the birds climbed out of the hollow which obscured their bodies, I saw from their plumage that they were all hens. Perhaps they included Steve's mate and his daughters.

To conclude this incident, let me say that in those long-ago days it was basic musketry advice that when shooting at a moving target – such as a mounted enemy – one aimed three feet ahead of the intended victim. In all modesty, let me also say that at that year's annual musketry at Filabusi from which Wallace and I were returning, I had retained the "crossed rifles" insignia of a B.S.A. Police marksman.

CHAPTER TWENTY-ONE
Cock's Farm

A sturdy gate across the track lined by the ostrich-damaged fence put an end to my recollection of various incidents concerning the ungainly birds. The gate and a glimpse of some corrugated iron roofing peeping through breaks in a plantation of gum trees in the distance told me that I had arrived at Cock's Farm. It was still early in the morning and about eight-thirty when I reached the plantation.

Dismounting, I loosened Charcoal's saddle-girth, removed the bit and crossed stirrups, finally tethering my mount to one of the saplings. Making Charcoal comfortable gave me the opportunity to examine the buildings around which there was little activity. From experience I had always found it useful to spy out the land before making my official presence known and, with the relatively serious case of the theft of as many as two dozen Black-headed Persian sheep before me, I reckoned there was nothing to be gained by barnstorming the place. My arrival had gone unnoticed and I had time to memorise the lay-out before I emerged.

I was still some distance from the dwelling when a fat African woman emerged from a side door carrying an enamel bucket. She was closely followed by a male African who broke off his conversation with the woman abruptly on seeing me. He changed direction, crossed the remains of a flower garden and greeted me with much bowing in a dialect which immediately revealed that he was from Northern Rhodesia. I replied in the Silozwe tongue and asked him where his morena was. Mr Cock, I was told, had left for Bulawayo at first light that morning. The boss-boy had been left in charge. I asked that the boss-boy be summoned, whereupon the house servant trotted off towards the cowshed where there were signs of activity. An African carrying a spade emerged from the shed in response to the house servant's call, there was a hurried whispered conversation and several glances in my direction and then the boss-boy leaned his spade against the gate, dusted off his hands on his overalls and hurried towards me.

Having exchanged greetings with the boss-boy, I dismissed the house servant and retraced the steps of the former back to the cattle shed where it became evident that I had interrupted the foreman in the task of cleaning out the dipping race in preparation for the cattle dipping the following day.

More interesting as far as I was concerned was the well constructed sheep kraal beyond the cattle dip. Its walls were of sandstone and a solid gate gave access from the cattle compound. On the opposite side of the kraal was an elaborate counting race made of gumpoles. Above the narrow passageway down which only one sheep could pass at a time, there was a solid platform, allowing the employee tasked with counting the sheep a comfortable seat.

I couldn't help thinking with some amusement that things had been made so easy for the checker that there was a real possibility of his "dropping off" – into sleep rather than from his perch above the livestock!

Climbing up into the checker's seat, I sat in authority to continue my questioning of the boss-boy. His accent had already identified him as hailing from the same parts as the house servant, his name was Josefa Lubinda and he had been employed at Cock's Farm for the relatively short period – to have risen to the position of boss-boy – of only ten months.

I switched to questioning him in Silozwi, a measure which not only produced a broad grin on the face of the subject but, more helpfully, produced more informative answers to my questions. Lubinda's rapid promotion was explained when he told me that he was only one of a whole gang of foreigners recruited and employed by Mr Cock. I moved on to question him about the sheep his employer had reported missing. He knew nothing, he said, volunteering that he did not herd the sheep. Another Mlozwi – Nasoni – was responsible for that chore and he was presently down in the valley with the flock. Lubinda waved his arm and from my vantage point I could see the very distinctively-marked animals, peacefully grazing some distance away.

"Who counts the sheep as they pass through this race?"

"I do, Morena," answered Lubinda.

"How often do you count them?"

"Daily," came the reply.

"Does Mr Cock ever count them?"

"Yes, he counts them at the end of every month."

"So who discovered the twenty missing?"

"Mr Cock – when he made the count a few days ago."

I now ceased my interrogation. Lubinda had made no attempt to explain how his daily count had failed to reveal a gradual loss of the two-dozen sheep. A sudden overnight loss would surely have been even more noticeable and it was likely that someone would have encountered the trail left by so many animals if someone from outside had driven off the sheep in one batch. Equally apparent in terms of this second possibility was the fact that 24 Black-headed Persians could not be spirited away in the rolling grazing country of the Bembesi Flats where their distinctive markings would have made them stand out like sore thumbs.

While the owner might shed more light on the disappearances, I was certain it was an "inside job". The presence of an alien clique also aroused my suspicions. While waiting for Mr Cock's return from Bulawayo, I decided to see what the Mlozwi shepherd had to say about the missing stock.

The absence in Bulawayo of the former owner of the two dozen Black-headed Persians was hampering my enquiries into the disappearance of the sheep. The foreman, Lubinda, couldn't explain how all the sheep had been accounted for one day and had been conspicuously absent the following day when Mr Cock himself had supervised the daily count. I was positive that 24 sheep could not have been driven off in one fell swoop and, while I had no supporting evidence, I was already more than a little suspicious of Lubinda and the other members of his Mlozwi clique. I seemed to be on a cold trail and Cock's absence did nothing to warm things up.

A curious thing happened before I took my leave of the boss-boy to stroll down into the valley and interrogate the shepherd, Nasoni. Blanco, my bull terrier, had been indulging in his usual form of recreation – that of chasing any form of wildlife generous enough to risk the dog's amusement. In this instance the fat lizards inhabiting the sandstone wall of the sheep kraal were the prey but they were far too nimble for Blanco and, by the time I had finished questioning Lubinda, my terrier had been reduced to a panting heap on the cool earth. As I closed my notebook and climbed down from the counting perch above the race, Blanco rose from his ridiculous sea lion posture, shook himself from head to tail and, with lowered head and a deliberate stalking motion, took up a threatening position behind the boss-boy. There he stood quivering, visibly ready to pounce on my word of command. Lubinda half-turned and became aware of Blanco's menacing attitude. Although he hadn't actually growled, his droopy bloodshot eyes and his tensed body left no doubt of his intent. To be wise after the fact, Blanco's wrinkled forehead and his obvious mistrust seemed to convey a combined order and insult: "Get out of my way, you damned liar!"

The foreman needed no more explicit command. He leapt for the perch I had just vacated and clung there quaking at the knees in harmony with the dog's quivering threat. A move to break the stalemate came when, with great presence of mind, Blanco slid under the lower horizontals of the race, very effectively barring his victim's only avenue of escape to the open veld. It all happened so quickly that for my part I could do little but watch. When I realised that the boss-boy – for no obvious reason – had been well and truly treed by Blanco, I walked towards the neighbouring cattle kraal, whistling my faithful hound to heel as I did so. Years later such partnership between a policeman and his dog might have been called intimidation. But rarely was any physical harm done in my day, while throwing a scare into a reluctant witness or a downright guilty party often paid dividends. In this instance I honestly felt I had given Blanco no cause for aggression. Admittedly I had my suspicions regarding Lubinda's position as leader of Mr Cock's imported labour but I had not the slightest hard evidence. Blanco, of course, did not have to provide chapter and verse before leaping to his own conclusions – pouncing on straws might be a better metaphor!

Blanco followed obediently if reluctantly in my wake and as I passed through the outer gate of the cattle kraal, he became resigned to not making an arrest for the time being. There would be other opportunities for him to show his stuff and until then he could don his other mask of playful pup – and let down his hair in every sense. But I couldn't get over the way he had acted.

"What's wrong, old chap? Don't you trust that bloke? You certainly put the wind up him." I ended the one-sided conversation with a peculiar chuckle which invariably brought forth from Blanco an unmistakeable expression of delight. The wrinkles on his forehead vanished and a broad grin – stretching from the base of one ear, through his wide-open mouth with its lolling tongue, to the base of the other ear – illustrated his good humour in no uncertain fashion. As we strode towards the open veld where Cock's remaining sheep were grazing, the prospect of putting up a rabbit or a meercat added that degree of anticipated excitement so dear to any dog born and bred in the districts.

Some five hundred yards down the valley were the grazing sheep – but no sign of their shepherd. I cupped my hands and yelled "Umfaan" and then, remembering his name from Lubinda's answer to my question, added "Nasoni". A black African head – not a Blackheaded Persian – popped up from the grass nearby. I beckoned. The herd-boy came very slowly and while he could have had no idea of what had transpired between the boss-boy and Blanco, he eyed the dog with ill-concealed trepidation. Not wanting to get off on the wrong foot, I told the nervous shepherd (with fingers crossed) that the dog wouldn't bite him. But still his approach was anything but swift. Eventually, keeping one eye on Blanco, he seated himself before me on a tuft of grass.

It came as no surprise to learn that Nasoni was another Mlozwi and after asking him how he came to be working for Mr Cock (he'd arrived in the same contingent as his fellow tribesmen), I moved on to the subject of the missing sheep. When had he first noticed that some of them had gone missing? Only when his employer had told him of the shortfall. Did he know the boss-boy Lubinda well and hadn't the boss-boy complained of the loss earlier – after his professed daily count – that a large number were missing? Yes and no were the respective answers. In reiteration, the first time that he'd known anything was wrong was when Mr Cock complained? Yes.

But Lubinda *did* count the sheep every day? Yes. And he'd never said that any were missing? No.

Nason's shepherding qualifications left much to be desired but he was adamant that none had strayed while he's been looking after them in the veld. I put to him the all important question: "Well, Nasoni, what has happened to the missing sheep?" Blanco pricked up his ears for the answer.

There was an uncomfortable silence, the shepherd's eyes flickering between my stern expression, Blanco's obvious air of distrust, the distant homestead and the kraals where Lubinda was most certainly concerned about what was taking place down among the sheep. Suddenly I reverted to Sindebele: "O la Manga!" ("You are a liar!")

Now perhaps as a proud owner I was inclined to overestimate Blanco's intelligence and detecting prowess but *manga* was a word he certainly understood. It was his signal to take up stance next to or behind the suspect with tail drooping threateningly and wagging with studied impatience, head sunk towards the ground and bloodshot eyes, wrinkled forehead and saliva-dripping, drooping jaws making very plain his threat of "Watch it!" It was the sort of nightmare cameo suffered after reading *Hounds of the Baskervilles* – even if Blanco's stature was considerably more modest than that of Conan Doyle's monsters.

Nasoni was suitable impressed. He took a last frightened look over his left shoulder at Blanco's undisguised belligerence, sidled imperceptibly away from the dog and spilled the beans.

"I didn't kill the sheep, *Nkoshe*. It was the boss-boy!"

"I knew you would speak the truth," I replied in his own language, unable to keep the satisfaction out of my response. "Now if you want to make a statement, I will write it down carefully. But I must warn you that if the case goes to court, anything you say now will be told to the magistrate. Do you understand what I am saying?"

"Oh, yes," responded Nasoni, seemingly relieved that everything was now out in the open. "I only want to tell the truth of what happened."

The spate of sheep-stealing had started some weeks before when the boss-boy had thumped the black head of one of the Persians with a knobkerrie as the fat and undoubtedly appetising animal had passed beneath him through the counting race. As Lubinda and the other Mlozwi had feasted for days on roast mutton, with no one apparently being aware of the crime, a second animal had been similarly despatched. Thereafter there was no satisfying the illegally acquired tastes of the foreman and his henchmen. Mutton became a regular and substantial item on the menu. Nasoni didn't comment when I expressed my amazement that as many as two dozen animals could have been slaughtered and eaten in as many days.

It was now necessary to substantiate the shepherd's story but he denied knowing anything of what had happened to the skins. He did however name the four gourmets besides Lubinda and himself and, confident that he wouldn't abscond, I instructed him to return to caring for his remaining flock.

When I returned to the homestead my constable had arrived with the pack animal, although there was still no sign of the complainant, Mr Cock. Having told the constable to make camp, I strolled over to the compound in which the accused had their quarters.

While searching the huts for traces of drying meat I still found it hard to believe that the six Mlozwi could have entirely consumed such a quantity of meat in addition to their normal rations – Blanco took himself off to investigate the potentially most interesting cache for a bull terrier, namely the ashpit. I followed his lead, having found nothing in the quarters, and discovered him gnawing a bone. Tiring of this burnt offering, Blanco then started scratching at the dead grey ash. Borrowing a spade from the gardener, I joined in on the excavations and after only a few minute of digging unearthed what was undeniably the skin of a Blackheaded Persian sheep. Summoning the constable to witness the find, and then taking turns with the spade, we soon uncovered more skins deeper in the ash.

At this stage I saw no reason why the constable and I should exhaust ourselves in most unpleasant and very dirty hard labour. Some of the employees, among them the guilty Mlozwi, were inspanned to uncover the hard evidence of their dirty deeds. Sixteen identifiable skins were recovered, some partially burnt, some very wilted and others in a very soggy sorry state.

Then began the tedious business of recording warned and cautioned statements but by mid-afternoon Lubinda and four of his fellow tribesmen and the incriminating evidence were en route to Fort Rixon under the watchful but very satisfied eyes of my constable, Blanco and myself.

When Mr Cock returned home that night he was somewhat taken aback to find his labour force considerably depleted. I'd left Nasoni to look after the remaining sheep – as my prime prosecution witness, he deserved some reward. An irate sheep farmer was on the phone to the station soon after my arrival there with my "bag". His indignation evaporated after having been informed officially of the facts and then re-appeared to a lesser degree when my sergeant requested his presence in court the following morning.

"Ye Gods!" he exclaimed. "You've taken all my labour force and now you want me as well!"

Lubinda and his four accomplices were duly sentenced –

Nasoni not being prosecuted because of his invaluable assistance in the prosecution of the case.

Mr Cock underwent a change of heart in regard to his preference for imported Mlozwi labour.

So ended my second successive and successful sheep-stealing case but, when it came to unofficial commendations, my own opinion was that Blanco had more than earned his colours for literally uncovering the mystery of the missing sheep – to say nothing of his skill in "questioning" witnesses.

CHAPTER TWENTY-TWO
From Business to Pleasure

Soon after the double success of stolen sheep, I was joined at Fort Rixon by an old schoolfriend, Jerry. Life became even more pleasant than before. Together we joined in the district's sporting life and attended dances at Shangani where I met a sweet girl who some years later was to become my wife.

I was assigned to accompany my old friend on his first patrol to show him the ropes and, while visiting a farmhouse in the early stages of the trip, we were invited to help ourselves from a heavily laden mulberry tree. Jerry, eager to sample the larger juicier fruits which were always just out of reach of more simply satisfied mortals, climbed the tree and for his pains unknowingly collected a large hairy caterpillar down the back of his shirt. We moved on to our next port of call but had not gone far before Jerry started to squirm and show signs of distress. I asked him what was wrong.

"There's something stinging my back," he replied.

"Let's stop and see what it is."

We dismounted and Jerry wasted no time stripping off his shirt. Examining his back I found a line of blisters running up his spine. The cause of the injury was still happily squirming in the folds of Jerry's shirt. We waited for the pack animals to catch up when I applied my universal panacea – lead and opium ointment – the use of which had saved me from much discomfort in the past although we carried it ostensibly to treat our animals' saddle sores. The treatment lessened Jerry's terrible itch and the burning sensation and we were able to proceed with the patrol.

Late in the afternoon we reached a delightful spot where we decided to camp for the evening. A local farmer quickly heard of our arrival and invited the two of us to his house for a game of bridge that evening. We thanked him and said we'd be along as soon as we had cleaned ourselves up and had something to eat.

Jerry's day of misadventure was far from over, however. As we were about to leave for the farmhouse with our torches to guide us, my companion decided to go off into the bush to relieve himself.

Whilst waiting for him, I heard Jerry cursing to himself.

"What's wrong this time?" I asked.

"Just come and see," came the agonised reply.

I strolled over to where he had disappeared into the darkness to find him in the light of my torch dancing from one foot to the other with his breeches about his ankles. Without going into precise anatomical details, what had happened was that a scorpion or other stinging insect had stung poor Jerry on the tip of his most vulnerable (if not valuable) piece of equipment. It was no time for modesty and as I examined the injury a blister grew almost to the size of a golf ball. It appeared to be no worse than a water blister but lead and opium seemed to me to be a rather harsh treatment in this instance and all I could do was to help Jerry into his pyjamas and put him to bed. Not wishing to disappoint our hosts, I went up to the farm, explained his absence, which was received with most unsympathetic hilarity, and then betrayed myself by thoroughly enjoying a game of three-handed bridge. I doubt if Jerry ever forgot his first patrol.

Another character gracing the Fort Rixon barrackrooms was Jimmy, at first sight a very independent type who knew all about life and who could be told nothing. But this was merely a front. Jimmy kept his ears wide open, was extremely gullible, and if someone said something in his hearing which interested him, he would want to know all the facts as soon as the narrator had left. Once Jimmy's colleagues had twigged onto his insatiable desire to know everyone else's business, it left him wide open to an unending series of pranks. One well-planned laugh at Jimmy's expense was built on his tremendous appetite – for food as well as every scrap of local scandal. Jimmy was still digging in heartily after his two companions, Doug and George, had long finished their meal when one of them surmised quietly to the other – but just loud enough for Jimmy to hear – that their hungry colleague was undoubtedly suffering from worms.

Squad 8/27 parading for the morning remount ride.
Trooper Palmer last on right   (Trevor Reed)

RSM 'Jock' Douglas   Mount Cazalet Gwanda

Gwanda Police Camp
1930

Trooper Palmer with Corporal White and local storekeeper Mr Robinson outside Fort Rixon Police Station 1930 The 1914 Model T Ford was used to collect mail from Insiza.

Mr Robinson, Corporal White and Trooper Palmer (Trevor Reed)

Trooper Palmer in centre with mail vehicle. Names of others unknown.

"What's that, old fellow? What did you say?" asked Jimmy anxiously.

"Oh, nothing much, Jimmy," replied Doug casually. "I was just saying to George here that from the way you eat you must have a case of worms!"

"Now that you mention it, Doug, I've been thinking the same thing." Hypochondria was typical of Jimmy's long list of peculiarities. "But what can I do about it?" he asked.

This was the crux of Doug and George's carefully-laid plan.

"Well, Jimmy," answered Doug hesitantly, "If you really want to be cured, we can fix you up."

"How, man? Just tell me how?" Jimmy couldn't wait for the answer to his imagined problem.

"The first thing is that you must starve yourself for 24 hours," advised Doug. "Eat nothing and drink only plain water. Then you must take a pill which I'll give you and that will get rid of the worms."

Jimmy was silent for a while, thinking over the rather "desperate" cure. Finally he spoke up. "I don't mind the pill part but I don't know how I'm going to be able to starve myself for 24 hours – that's the hard part."

"Well, that's it then," said Doug, dismissing the whole idea. But Jimmy was worried. "Couldn't we see if it works after only a 12 hour fast?" he queried. "I reckon I could just about manage that long."

"We'll give it a go, then," agreed Doug.

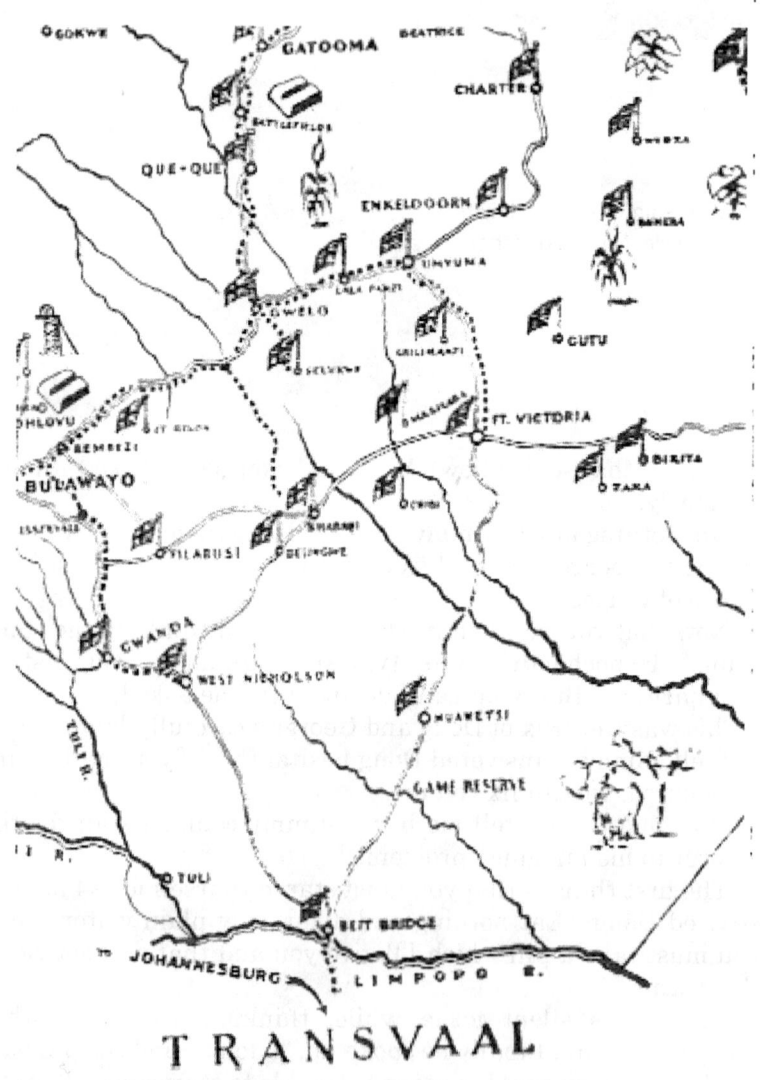

Map showing the various locations of Trooper Palmer's stories

Jimmy swallowed the last bit of food he was to get for 12 hours and then dutifully swallowed the green, liquid-encased-in-gelatine pill which Doug generously proffered. Had the victim been slightly more knowledgeable, he would have recognised the medication for what it was – a pill normally used when a horse was suffering from worms.

The result was predictable. Jimmy just about lived in the toilet for the next few days. What was more pathetic was that each time he returned to the barrack room he would sorrowfully announce that he had been unable to discover any worms in the bucket. The joke, far from innocent at the beginning, soured considerably. Jimmy became so weak and dehydrated that the sergeant-in-charge thought it wise to call in the G.M.O. The latter gave Doug and George a thorough dressing down for their foolishness, the reprimand being couched in anything but medical terminology! By the time he'd finished, the guilty pair were relieved only to the extent of being told that the matter would not be taken further.

Doug and George did not learn their lesson. Soon afterwards Jimmy came upon the pair of pranksters standing on the edge of a mat on the veranda vying with each other to see how far each in turn could push a large basin of water between his legs from a stooping position. Again, it had all been planned in advance and, just as predictably, Jimmy could not restrain his curiosity. He wanted to know what was going on. Doug patiently explained the rules of the game, carefully not inviting Jimmy to participate. Of course, Jimmy could not be left out in the cold.

"I can do much better than either of you," he claimed. "After all, I've got longer legs."

"No," said George. "This contest is just between Doug and me."

Their refusal only increased Jimmy's frustration. Finally they agreed to let him try and beat their chalk marks. Jimmy, doubled over like a piece of string on the edge of the mat, was just pushing the basin beyond the jokers' marks when they seized the other end of the mat and yanked it violently. He toppled backwards with some force, landing bottom first in the basin of cold water. His tormentors roared with laughter.

"I suppose you thought that was funny!" said Jimmy as he took himself off to change into another pair of trousers.

Perhaps anyone of us would have fallen for the next episode of Doug and George's continual devilment – but Jimmy had to be the victim again. Knowing that Jimmy was within earshot inside the barrack room one morning Doug grabbed George and yelled: "Watch out! There's a snake!" On cue, George jumped in alarm and took refuge on the tabletop like a mouse-frightened housewife. Jimmy burst into the room.

"Where's the snake? – let me get at it – I'm not afraid of snakes!"

"There in the corner," answered Doug. "Can't you see it?"

As poor old Jimmy peered into the dimly-lit corner of the room, George leaned over from the tabletop and pricked the victim in the leg with two pins held in his fingers. Once again, Jimmy's reaction was as expected.

"Help!" he yelled. "I've been bitten!"

The non-existent snake was forgotten and Jimmy hobbled off to his bed where the two pranksters insisted that the wound be immediately cauterised. Jimmy was brutally operated upon with a penknife, and iodine and potash were rubbed into the four cuts inflicted, just to make sure that Jimmy suffered as though he had really been bitten by a snake. This incident, fortunately, didn't get as far as the GMO – perhaps because they were afraid of a second tongue-lashing (and payment in kind for their mischief at a later date from the medical officer). They confided in the sergeant and when Jimmy reported sick later, he examined the wound, pronounced that it looked as though Doug and George's prompt "treatment" had saved the day, and advised Jimmy not to see the G.M.O. unless the condition of his leg worsened.

But Jimmy was not always so foolish and, being generous in hindsight, I wonder if on occasions he didn't realise only too well that he was being taken for a ride but played along with the prank for the sake of enlivening the sometimes dull existence of a district station.

I have already mentioned "The Warlord", the district's police superintendent, and his lordship's predilection for full-scale military exercises. Jimmy featured prominently in one such exercise and emerged with flying colours as far as his colleagues were concerned. The Warlord's commendation was a great deal longer in being awarded.

The "target" was an imaginary machine-gun nest on the summit of a kopje.

"I shall lead the attack with sword drawn and I want you men to storm after me with fixed bayonets and dislodge the enemy," announced our fearless leader. "Ready? Charge!!!"

The more compliant members of the Warlord's command

huffed and puffed their way up the hillside, yelling obscenely at the imaginary enemy and obeying their officer's order to make the exercise as realistic as possible.

Not so Jimmy. On reaching a stormdrain at the foot of the hill he flopped onto the long grass growing in the drain and watched with no little amusement as his colleagues laboured into the attack. Jimmy stayed in the drain until the Warlord returned from the successful foray and discovered one of his men comfortably stretched out on the grass.

"What's the meaning of this?" roared the irate commander.

Jimmy looked up, his face took on a pained expression.

"I've been wounded, sir. Are there no stretcher bearers to carry me back to camp?"

The Warlord stamped and cursed with a degree of energy quite surprising after his charge up the kopje. Jimmy's only response was – "Well, you did say we have to make the exercise as realistic as possible, sir!"

Another occasion on which Jimmy proved to his mates that he was not the fool he sometimes appeared to be was when the Warlord, despite his previous encounter with his "wounded" subordinate, had Jimmy appointed as his orderly for a tour of police camps in the district. The Warlord's safari was organised in a fashion completely typical of the man. Camp would be made for the night in the veld so that "surprise" early morning raids could be mounted on unsuspecting members-in-charge. But the secret itinerary was compromised to the extent that his lordship insisted that his newspapers and mail be available for collection at dawn at predetermined points. Thus one morning found Jimmy setting the table and preparing his superior's breakfast while the latter sat back and read the newspaper at some lonely spot in the bush.

Jimmy announced that breakfast was ready and the Warlord looked up to see that two places had been set at the table. Very deliberately he raised his monocle to his eye, looked at the two places set at the table and then at Jimmy and coldly observed: "Trooper, what do you think the Commissioner would say if he arrived at this moment?"

Jimmy was equal to the occasion. Foraging in the well-stocked box of foodstuffs which always accompanied the inspection tour, he replied quite seriously: "I shouldn't worry, sir. There's plenty here for the Commissioner as well as for us!"

The Warlord was once again lost for a suitable reply.

The last I heard of Jimmy was that he had landed in hospital in Salisbury after having been attacked and mauled by a lion somewhere in Mashonaland.

He had been saved by his constable who had bravely attacked the wounded lion with nothing more than an axe.

CHAPTER TWENTY-THREE
Waterworks

Returning to Fort Rixon one day, I noticed a great deal of activity taking place at the well which served the camp. In charge of a gang of labourers was Bunny, the son of a local farmer I knew well. Before off-saddling, I rode over to see what was going on.

Bunny explained that he had been given the contract to sink a new sixty-foot well to bolster the camp's rather erratic water supply. He and his men had been at it for three or four days and had found the going very difficult. The ground was so hard that even the hand drilling of holes for dynamite charges was proving a very slow process. Out of curiosity, I asked Bunny why he had chosen this particular site.

"It's all to do with the formation of the barrier reef coming down from the kopje," he explained. "I reckon we'll strike water eventually, but it's hard work – I'm using seventy-five per cent gelignite to blast the overburden out."

To me this sounded very professional but I wondered aloud about the accuracy and results of using the legendary forked-stick method of water divining. Bunny – the professional – intimated that he had little faith in such "superstitious" means of finding water, an attitude I didn't share having had no small success with the proverbial forked stick at Mazunga. When I argued with Bunny on the basis of my experience, quite predictably he accepted the challenge.

"Well, Palmer, if you were able to find water in a desert like Mazunga, you're more than welcome to try here."

Borrowing a small axe from a labourer, I cut a Y-shaped stick from a nearby green bush which was growing in formerly cultivated land where one of the constables had grown a mealie crop. I instructed Bunny to blindfold me and to then lead me across the area in question in four different directions. At the point at which the pull on my forked stick was strongest, I asked that a stone be placed. When I uncovered my eyes, even I was surprised to see that the four stones were within inches of each other.

"This is where you must dig, Bunny. I'm sure you will find a strong underground stream at this point."

There was no mistaking Bunny's scepticism, especially as my chosen site was some distance from where his men had been struggling for days. But I didn't press the point and rode off to the stables, leaving Bunny to take my advice or spurn it.

Something must have cropped up to take my mind off the well-digging operation over the next three or four days. After this period, Bunny walked into my office one morning and, to my surprise, slapped a government cheque for £60 under my eyes.

"What's this for?" I asked in astonishment.

"That's for sinking the new well. What's more, I suggest that you and I go into partnership – you be the dowser and I'll dig the wells. We'll make a fortune!"

I burst out laughing at Bunny's suggestion and his unsuppressed enthusiasm for the venture.

"I'm serious," he countered. "We really would make a good business team."

"What do you mean?" I asked, still a little mystified.

"Look at that cheque – sixty quid for a twenty-six-foot well! So much water came in at that depth that we couldn't cope with it. But the contract was for a sixty-foot well at a pound a foot." He leaned over and whispered more confidentially. "And what's more, I used only ten per cent gelignite – the cheapest on the market – whereas before you changed my mind about where to dig, I was using the most expensive blasting material."

"So you took my advice after all," I said with more than a hint of satisfaction.

"Yes," replied Bunny. "And I was pleased I'd done so almost as soon as we'd turned the first shovelful of earth. The soil was so soft that we could have sunk the well scarcely using picks – let alone explosives – right down to the water level."

"Well, Bunny, I'm glad my mystic powers were of some assistance to you and to improving the camp water supply. But I think I'll stick to my present job for the time being."

Years later I succeeded in dowsing for water at cattle sites in Botswana on numerous occasions.

Water at Fort Rixon had always been a problem. Even when there was enough water in the well, it had to be drawn to the surface by windlass and bucket. The water was then poured into the water-cart which was drawn by two oxen to the various points at which it was required. One of the most important requirements was water for the horses and mules and it was the responsibility of the person in charge of the water-cart to see that the troughs were filled each morning and afternoon. Next stop was the barrack room with its two tanks – one for the hot water system and one for the cold. Then there were the requirements of the NCOs' quarters and the native constables – all in all enough to keep the water-cart, and the person in charge of it, on the move for a few hours every day.

Unfortunately we didn't have the right man for the job. The incumbent came by courtesy of the Native Department – a character who had evaded his hut tax for eleven years and who, in the opinion of the Native Commissioner, was unlikely to cough up the back taxes while languishing in jail. In his wisdom the Native Commissioner had asked the Fort Rixon Police to employ the man at the princely wage of thirty shillings per month, two-thirds of which would be deducted to pay off the taxes.

The scheme wasn't of the best even if our press-ganged "Gunga Din" had been a reasonable type, accepting his sentence with good grace. But Mbanje was born lazy and the trouble we had getting him to perform his essential but not particularly onerous duties was never-ending. He would lose the two oxen and a sore toe would prevent him from going to look for them; if he did find them, a headache or a sore stomach would halt his activities; one day it would be too hot and the next day would be too cold for him to work.

Mbanje's excuses were legion and we were the sufferers because, thanks to the Native Commissioner, we could not dispense with his services until the back taxes had been paid. As Senior Trooper at Fort Rixon, Mbanje's conduct was a particular thorn in my side. My administrative responsibilities were added to by the fact that I had passed the B.S.A. Police language examination and was studying for the advanced Civil Service qualification and thus became the chief complaints officer not only for the constables but also the grazing guards and the camp followers. To mix a few metaphors, whenever there was a break in the pipeline, I got it in the neck – until I was sick to the teeth of the name Mbanje.

Came the great day when Mbanje paid his last instalment and we were at liberty to find a reliable replacement. No such luck!

Mbanje, realising he was on to a good thing, took up residence in the witnesses' quarters and was feeding himself on government rations – or so I was told. After interrogating the native corporal in charge of the lines, I learned that Mbanje was actually sleeping in the detention cells and – believe it or not – keeping himself warm at night with blankets taken from genuine prisoners. Efforts to remove Mbanje from the premises had been unsuccessful – although privately I wondered how insistent the native corporal had been. It was evident that the "stowaway" would have to be scared off, one way or another. I told the corporal that I would carry out an inspection of the lines and the cells the following morning.

As usual Blanco accompanied me on my rounds. My bull-terrier enjoyed the experience although he seldom caused any trouble when imitating, more literally, my own sniffing around the huts to see that all was in order. All went well until we arrived at the detention cells – by which time shining black faces were peering round every hut door in anticipation of the fun they were about to witness. They did not wait for long.

As I stopped at the entrance to the first cell, I was almost knocked flying by the naked but blanket-wrapped Mbanje. His indecent haste was emphasised in his speed of passage as the blanket fanned out behind him. Blanco needed no invitation.

The dog's immediate target was naturally the blanket and Mbanje qualified for an entry in the record book as one of Rhodesia's first "streakers". His discomfiture raised a roar of laughter from the onlookers which was heard at the Native Department's offices half-a-mile away. Blanco was only momentarily distracted from the chase in the recovery of one government blanket and was soon hard on the heels of the fleeing Mbanje.

At this stage I began to worry about the consequences and yelled for Blanco to come to heel. Either the excitement was too much for him or the yelling from the spectators drowned my shouts, but Blanco paid no attention. Mbanje's frightened glances over his shoulder at his pursuer only heightened the audience's enjoyment.

But our retreating waterworks supervisor had the last word – in a manner of speaking. Blanco, perhaps believing the unusual chase was all in fun, drew alongside his victim instead of snapping at his heels and Mbanje, either by accident or design, delivered the most timely water supply of his undistinguished career. As the stream of urine washed across Blanco's muzzle, the dog almost halted in midstride with an utterly disgusted look on his face and, a second later, was ploughing his muzzle into a tuft of grass in an effort to rid himself of the evil-smelling fluid.

That was the last we saw of Mbanje although at some stage he must have sneaked back to recover his clothes which I had instructed be placed at the point at which he had disappeared into the bush.

It was as well that he stayed away from Fort Rixon police camp. I don't think Blanco would have forgotten or forgiven the insult to which he'd been subjected.

CHAPTER TWENTY-FOUR
Hunting Hilarity

Most policemen of my era enjoyed a hunt during the weekends or whenever the opportunity presented itself. Besides, the occasional duiker or steenbuck made a change from the Fort Rixon diet of chicken and mutton and also helped to keep our mess bills down.

This is what my friend Jerry had in mind when he bought himself a 7.4mm sporting rifle, a weapon of which he was very proud and with which he was anxious to display his prowess. The opportunity only arose when a clerk in the Native Department passed on the news that a gang of prisoners, out searching for firewood, had spotted a reed buck quite close to the camp. Jerry sought and was given permission to try out his new toy.

The prison gang and their guard accompanied Jerry on the foray and they came across the buck grazing quietly in the vlei very close to where it had first been seen. Jerry wasted no time and his first shot broke one of the animal's hind legs. It leapt into the air and made off, slowed considerably by the one limp and dangling leg. The hunting party set out in pursuit.

Now it so happened that one of the convicts was a Nyasa and a devout Muslim with – it might be said – an equally devout eye to the future. In short, if he was to partake of his share of the spoils, it had to be despatched on the hoof in the prescribed manner dictated by the Koran. So Jerry's second shot at the buck was postponed by an axe-brandishing Nyasa who sprinted across Jerry's field of fire in hot pursuit of the injured animal.

The buck, not surprisingly confused, crossed the Fort Rixon-Shangani road and headed for the Native Department offices. There the two clerks had heard the shot and needed no second bidding to drop their work and find out exactly what was happening. First on the scene was the wounded reed buck, then came the axe-waving Muslim, another two prisoners were close behind and also armed with hatchets, while their jailer valiantly tried to keep up with his charges with his Martini-

Henry bouncing at the Regimental slope. Jerry brought up the rear with his 7.4mm rifle at the trail and an assortment of bodies between him and his target. It was quite a procession.

The reed buck next crossed the track leading to the local store and then came up against the fence surrounding the Native Commissioner's garden. Bursting through a barrier not designed to keep out frenzied animals, the buck limped up the drive past the house where the local squire's lady was knitting on the stoep. She could hardly be blamed for dropping a stitch or two as the wounded buck careered across her garden with a blood-thirsty jailbird in pursuit. She regained her senses, if not her composure, in time to tack onto the rear of the chase, waving her knitting needles in annoyance at the intrusion on her privacy.

Turning a bend in the drive, the buck limped swiftly back in the direction of the Native Department offices where the two clerks, wild with excitement, were yelling "ten to one on the buck" as the various hunters panted past them. Next point on the tour was the jail just beyond the administrative offices. By this time the Native Commissioner, who was debriefing his chief messenger, realised that some sort of commotion was taking place, armed himself with his heavy ebony ruler and hobbled to the doorway. The head messenger, rather quicker off the mark, sprinted to cut off the buck – in time to collect the commissioner-flung ruler on the side of the head, the missile dislodging the messenger's headgear and causing him to clap his hands to his temple in pain.

The buck continued on its merry way – for the spectators at least – until it ran into an old man who was treating skins behind the jail. The animal butted the *madala* fair and square in the stomach and then collapsed in a heap on top of the old man – at about the same time as the two Native Department clerks collapsed, weak with laughter, on their grandstand.

Jerry was never allowed to forget his first hunt with the new rifle but whether or not the Muslim – who had played such a leading role in the comedy – ever received his hard-earned share of the meat is lost in the mists of time.

There were certainly leopards in the hills around Fort Rixon but in all the years I was stationed there the only time lions were mentioned was when one of the troopers named Ray came into the camp at top speed and announced that he had seen no less than five "kings of the jungle" just outside the village. Ray collected his rifle and several additional self-professed crack shots and dashed off to the Nellie Mine. The "lions" turned out to be only a pair of cheetah so another grand hunting session came to nought.

Mention of the cheetah reminds me of more fun and games at Fort Rixon, an incident in which I played – on reflection – a rather irresponsible role.

I remember I had bought a cheetah skin from an African who had successfully trapped the animal after it had killed one of his newly born calves. He had "cured" the skin with an unusual combination of fats and in an effort to get rid of the unpleasant odour, I hung the skin on the hitching rail outside the barrack room. The horses were grazing on the edge of the square and either the smell or the appearance of the skin itself as it flapped in the wind made them inquisitive. They approached the hitching rail cautiously, snorting and whinneying their curiosity. And then a particularly heavy gust of wind made the skin flap loudly and, as one, the horses bolted for the other side of the square where they turned, snorted their disgust and pawed the ground. Jerry and I watched their antics for a while until I took the skin inside to let our mounts graze in peace.

It was some days later that I decided to have some fun. Slipping the skin under my shirt, I called Blanco and together we strolled down to the storeroom next to the horse lines. There I draped the cheetah skin about the dog's body and secured it. The skin was so big that the head flopped over Blanco's eyes while the tail and hindquarters dragged behind. Stable parade was in progress with the constables reluctantly grooming the horses. I commanded Blanco to "stay" and walked casually to the other end of the lines. Then I whistled for my dog.

Blanco burst out of the store, his wagging tail threshing the skin from side to side in a fair old imitation of a cheetah rushing its prey. In an instant there was bedlam up and down the lines as horses reared and lashed out in all directions. The panic spread right down to the mule lines, halters and reins were broken, and in a short space of time the lines were devoid of a single piece of horseflesh. The constables were picking themselves up from where they had been scattered as their charges bolted with hooves flying.

It took a considerable time to round up all the animals and even longer to lead them past the store from which the "cheetah" had burst without warning. For my part I fully deserved the ticking-off I received from the Member-in-Charge who, at that particular time, could well do without the pranks his irresponsible troopers were getting up to.

We were unfortunate enough to have the country home of the Prime Minister, Howard Moffat at Shangani in our area and one afternoon, when I was lucky enough to be out on patrol, a report was received that an African had been caught trying to steal the PM's shotgun. While the offence itself was serious, there was no panic as the culprit had been apprehended. It was merely a question of sending someone out to Shangani to collect the accused. The only policeman immediately available to answer the summons was a constable suffering from a sore foot – and also a relative newcomer to Fort Rixon. Getting lost on his way to his destination further crippled a prompt police presence and our reputation was not enhanced by the fact that the accused managed to escape before the constable arrived – although the shotgun had been safely recovered by the farm manager. The constable did his best to search for the culprit but the latter had a head start and, as mentioned, the constable had a "footnote" to handicap his tailing of the offender.

The outcome of the whole affair was that the Prime Minister, not "in residence" at Shangani at the time, received only his displeased manager's version of the story and lodged a complaint with the Commissioner of Police. So it was that the District Superintendent was charged with investigating the whole affair and particularly the insinuation of inefficiency against the Fort Rixon sergeant-in-charge. It even went as far as a magistrate's hearing at Fort Rixon but thankfully the sergeant was completely exonerated and served on to earn not only his pension but also the long service and good conduct medal to which he was fully entitled.

This minor incident, blown up out of all proportion, was largely responsible for my reluctance to seek promotion – although I was officially "advised" to do so.

For the time being at least, I much preferred to remain a humble trooper.

CHAPTER TWENTY-FIVE
Beitbridge

Twelve months after the unpleasantness between Prime Minister Moffat and my sergeant-in-charge at Fort Rixon, I reconsidered my earlier reservations about advancement, went to Salisbury where I sat and passed my promotion examinations and then returned to Fort Rixon to await a new posting. The transfer came before my stripes and I was returned to my old haunts on the Limpopo, this time as Trooper-in-Charge at Beitbridge. The bridge itself had been opened the previous year (1929) and at last the authorities were getting round to constructing a police station befitting the increasingly important "port" of entry. While the builders got on with the new station, I had to take up residence in the old camp.

It was a ramshackle place perched on top of a hill. My duties were varied, to say the least, the usual police work relegated to low priority among immigration and post office duties, including the sending and receipt of telegrams.

Immigration checks were pleasant enough when one's clients were returning residents, but there were large numbers of immigrants in those depressed years, job-seekers who lacked the qualifications for entry or had insufficient funds to prevent them from becoming a burden on Rhodesia's stretched finances. The latter had to be painfully turned away.

There was also an influx of would-be wildebeeste hunters, the blue-skinned gnu having been declared vermin because of the disease it spread when grazing among ranch cattle. The "sportsmen" came with no more than rifles, ammunition and a bag of mealie meal and were surprised when we looked less than kindly upon them. The hunters and the bands of relatives they brought with them were interested in nothing more than shooting game and making biltong. Vermin of another sort had a more pleasant outcome.

I tried to bath at least once a day but my "bathroom" – a section of the veranda screened off with reeds – was itself alive with lice. No matter how hard I tried to fumigate the place there seemed to be no answer to the problem. I knew there must be a breeding ground somewhere and closer examination of the tall undergrowth growing right up against the building revealed an old 1918-model Chevrolet abandoned among the weeds. The hood of the vehicle had long since collapsed and the seats were thick with fowl droppings. The car had become the nesting box of every chicken in the native police lines.

My first step was to purchase the livestock wholesale and resign myself to a diet of chicken day in and day out. Then I managed to trace the owner of the car by means of its Salisbury number plate. It belonged to the Civil Commissioner in Fort Victoria. I wrote to him and he was delighted to hear that I had found a buyer for the wreck who was willing to pay £20 to take it off his – and my – hands.

The history of how the ancient Chevy came to be parked at the old Limpopo police camp was simply that the Civil Commissioner had returned from holiday in South Africa but while crossing the drift (long before the bridge had been completed), water had seeped into the petrol feed and he had been obliged to have the car towed by oxen to the camp.

Moving the wreck from beside my bathroom presented its own problems but one morning I gathered all available camp personnel, including prisoners, witnesses, labourers, constables and camp followers; took charge of the steering wheel and gave the order to push. The tyres were in shreds and the engine had been left in gear, in which state it had become thoroughly rusted up. Despite the numerical strength of my helpers, the task was no easy one. The only thing in our favour was that the Chevy was parked on a slight rise. We grunted and heaved and as the old bus gathered momentum down the hill, it actually gave a splutter and a cough and spluttered into life, albeit on only two or three cylinders. I leapt frantically for the running board and plonked my posterior in several years accumulation of fowl manure. To roars of applause from my helpers, the dilapidated old vehicle jerked and ground its way to the stables where with a tremendous bang it gave up the ghost. At least I'd removed the lousy breeding ground to a safe distance.

It was strange that after all the years of disuse, the car should have burst into life. The chap who bought it slaved for weeks but never managed to get as much as a kick out of the engine. He ended up dismantling it and selling it piecemeal for spares.

It was ironic that one of my last duties at Fort Rixon had been to set in motion the formalities surrounding the desertion of an alien worker from one of the local farms. About all one could do was to inform the Aliens Bureau at CID Bulawayo who in turn would warn the various border posts on the off chance that the deserter made an official exit from the country. One of my first duties at Beitbridge was to be on the receiving end of similar such notification.

A lengthy telegram from CIDHQ in Bulawayo gave a full description of a European chemist who had disappeared from Bulawayo and was believed to be heading for the border in a small Fiat motorcar. No record of the vehicle having passed through the border gate came to light and a few days after receiving the message I rode out on horseback some five miles from the station – for a few hours of peace and quiet rather than for any more specific reason. I came across the Fiat completely abandoned in the bush. A thorough search of the area proved fruitless and eventually the car was returned to the missing man's wife in Bulawayo. It must have been a sad message for the deserted woman but under financial stress – as the chemist had apparently been – there was no telling what a person would do.

It was assumed that the man had crossed the border on foot, the South African Police were asked to keep a watch for him and the case was filed until such time as the man was located or assumed to be dead.

The opening of the bridge had meant an influx of contractors and officials of the Public Works Department. In turn this meant there was a tremendous increase in the number of telegrams I was expected to handle – the minor boom in the village seemed to have upgraded all communication far beyond the ordinary mail! Sending the messages to Salisbury became virtually a full morning's work and the replies took up most of the afternoon. It was obvious that I needed some assistance. Not only was the telephone very old and the line indistinct at the best of times, but having relayed the messages and repeated them for accuracy to my link at Gwanda Post Office, it was then my responsibility to deliver the replies to the various officials who had descended upon Beitbridge.

For once the authorities got their priorities right and a sergeant was sent down to take over from me. This suited me fine – the sergeant took over the administrative responsibilities (including the communications link) and left me to get on with the more satisfying task of such police investigations as were necessary and even the odd bit of patrolling. I was more than happy to be given a measure of freedom.

I even managed to get a few days off one weekend and decided to take my rifle and visit my old happy hunting ground on the Limpopo river. Surprisingly quickly, my police tracker and I picked up the spoor of five or six kudu bulls. We followed the trail into mountainous ground – for that part of the country, that is – with a strong wind blowing in our faces.

Kudu have an acute sense of hearing but the high wind was blowing the trees about as we stalked and sighted the small herd. The first warning they had of our presence was my first shot which felled a bull standing on a boulder and making a perfect target. Strangely enough, the place of the collapsed bull was taken by another – they were in such a quandary they didn't know which way to bolt. Actually I thought I was firing at the same animal with my second shot which turned out to be a hit in the lungs. The animal bounded off some forty yards before keeling over stone dead.

Following up on my shots, I was surprised to find I had bagged two bulls at the shoulder in addition to the one who had run the short distance before dying. The double kill with my first shot was explained by the fluke that the bullet had passed through the heart of my target – and into the neck of a second animal lower down and behind the first. The three carcasses presented something of a problem – with enough meat to feed a regiment for several days, how was I to transport the dead kudu back to the camp?

The only solution was a second safari from the police camp utilising all six donkeys on the station strength. The going, over the hilly country, was not easy but there were no complaints from the constables who now had no lack of meat to go with their sadza for the better part of two weeks, with a goodly supply of biltong into the bargain. For myself, I wasn't particularly proud of my first fluke shot which had turned an already too easy hunt into what was virtually wholesale slaughter.

A few months went by and I was beginning to enjoy being stationed at Beitbridge. There was plenty of variety among the inhabitants as the various contractors came and went. The hotel was completed and then more slowly the residential quarters for the expected government officials were built. They were fast changing times with little chance for boredom to set in.

I should have realised that my happy lot would not last long. I was suddenly recalled to Fort Rixon for rather unusual reasons.

It seemed that the growing band of youngsters in Fort Rixon took exception to the local Lord of the Manor – the Native Commissioner. The discontent culminated in a raid on his lordship's castle one night when stones were rained on the tin roof causing so much panic among the elderly couple that they were almost convinced that the Third Matabele Rebellion had broken out. I suppose I should have been flattered that the Native Commissioner went as far as asking the District Superintendent that I be transferred back to Fort Rixon. Perhaps he thought I would have a stabilising influence on the rowdy youngsters. As it happened, my return to Fort Rixon was to be shortlived. No sooner had I settled down there than an appeal for CID applicants was circulated. I applied half-seriously and was completely surprised when the next I heard was that I should proceed to Bulawayo for an interview.

I did not go immediately to CIDHQ as I had become involved in the investigation of a rather unusual case.

CHAPTER TWENTY-SIX
Language and Lip Service

Sandy Adams was a Fort Rixon general dealer who sent a message to the station one day to complain that a servant to whom he'd given money for the purchase of cattle had converted some of the funds to his own use. As quite a large sum was involved, naturally he wanted the police to investigate.

Adams was a thick-set Scotsman who stood well over six feet in height. Originally he had been a mine captain at the Nelly Mine where he had met with an accident, losing a leg as a result. That put an end to his mining career and he hobbled around the district trying his hand at anything that could be interpreted as "general dealing" in the widest sense in order to make an honest living. He spoke in a broad accent which was liberally scattered with the choicest of adjectives picked up in the mines.

I went out to his place to sort out the matter, mentioning at the outset that I'd come to investigate a case of alleged theft by conversion.

I was greeted heartily and with a handshake which all but crushed my fingers.

"Aye, and I hope ye get the b------ for theft by conversation!"

Thereafter, and despite all my attempts to correct him, it was to remain a case of "theft by conversation" as far as Sandy was concerned.

Slowly and patiently I took down a statement of complaint, not only having to translate from broad Scots but having to censor in no small degree the miner's profanity in order to get the case started in an acceptable fashion. But there was little doubt that Sandy had been defrauded and eventually the case came up before the magistrate at Fort Rixon. The complainant turned up for the hearing in an old ram shackle car driven by his coloured son. For the great occasion he wore a large Stetson and a tie that was twisted halfway round his neck. To complete the picture for the prosecutor, Sandy was more than half-drunk – with the greater portion of a bottle of brandy in his pocket to complete his intoxication at the earliest opportunity.

Neither did Sandy see any reason to remove his pipe, which was rarely far from his mouth, on entering the courtroom. I told him smoking was not permitted and reluctantly he stuffed the pipe into his pocket – only to fumble for both pipe and matches, purely from habit, a few minutes later. As the proceedings commenced I again and again told Sandy that the magistrate did not allow smoking in court and each time he would reply in a very audible voice – "Why the hell not?" There was no point in telling him what contempt of court was or of the fine he laid himself open to should he get the magistrate's back up.

This was only the start of the courtroom fun and games. When Sandy was called to give evidence he hobbled across to the witness stand where he made himself comfortable on one crutch and waited for the prosecutor's questions in a manner no different to the frequent occasions on which Sandy held court in the local pub. One of the first rather superfluous questions was did Sandy know the accused.

"Och, aye, I know the b—! He worked for me until we nabbed the thievin' b— for theft by conversation. And here the b— is, lying through his thievin' teeth. He ought to get six months' bleedin' hard labour twice a bleedin' year!"

At this stage the magistrate asked the prosecutor to tell his chief witness to moderate his language or he would be forced to adjourn the case. When this was suitably translated for Sandy's benefit his reply was that this was the way he always bleedin' well spoke!

Before the magistrate could dream up a counter to this evident truth, Sandy spied a native messenger in the doorway.

"Iwe – you at the door – *manzi!*"

Now whether the messenger in question had experienced Scots temperament in the past or not, I don't know, but without hesitating he disappeared out of the door to return in what seemed like a few moments with a half-gallon white enamel bucket full of water – which he duly handed to the occupant of the witness stand. Before the dumb-founded magistrate and court officials, Sandy gulped down a goodly portion of the contents and poured the rest over his head and shoulders. He then addressed himself to the bench: "Och, that's better, yer wership. Noo ye can carry on!"

Fortunately, it was time for mid-morning tea – during which the magistrate and prosecutor pondered the merits of allowing the case to continue. The prosecutor, wise to Sandy's ways, pointed out that justice – and the dignity thereof – would be best served by getting on with the case before the complainant had a chance to fortify himself still further for the ordeal he was inflicting upon the court with a liquid lunch or, worse still, an overnight stop at the Insiza Hotel and its convenient and "fluid" bar hours for residents.

So the case was concluded – although the sentence remained to be ratified by the attorney general in view of the large sum of money involved. Because I had already been notified of my transfer to CID in Bulawayo, I knew I wouldn't be seeing Sandy Adams again and said farewell. Once again my hand came near to being crushed and almost as predictable was Sandy's parting shot – he was well into celebrating his courtroom victory.

"Well, Palmerr, we got the b— – hic – for theft by conversation, didn't we? Good luck to you, mon."

And that was the last I saw of one of Rhodesia's really hard cases. But a real character for all that.

One of my trickier assignments during the period of limbo at Fort Rixon while awaiting orders to report to Bulawayo originated with the Native Commissioner. One of his messengers who had been returning from visiting a kraal was found unconscious at the side of the road. The injured man was picked up by a passing car, brought into the village and given first aid treatment for a badly lacerated upper lip before being packed off to Bulawayo to receive proper medical attention. All the victim could remember was that he had been cycling down a steep hill at speed ... and the next he knew he was being brought into the village in someone's car in a sorry state. It would have been easy to write the matter off as a simple accident but for some reason the Native Commissioner had his doubts and asked for an investigation. I went out to the scene of the accident with a native constable – the lightest I could find – riding on the pillion.

With little trouble we located the scene and there, in the middle of the road, was a stone about the size of a cricket ball. The lump of rock stood out even in the surrounding gravel and closer examination showed that it had only recently been unearthed from its bed of fairly soft soil. It certainly was not a dislodged portion of the road's formation, nor did it seem likely that it had been thrown up from the verge. The constable and I did some careful sleuthing in the surrounding bush and then struck gold in a deep storm water drain which ran parallel with the road. Almost opposite where the stone had been found was a hole in the side of the drain into which the missile –for such it now appeared to be – fitted exactly. Closer examination indicated that someone had been squatting in the drain for some time. It looked very much as though the messenger had been ambushed – some enemy had been waiting for him to come down the hill, had thrown the stone with remarkable accuracy and had almost succeeded in killing the cyclist. Close examination of the stone showed what appeared to be moustache hairs clinging to one of its sharp sides.

Proving the theory would be a much more difficult proposition but my transfer came through before that aspect of the investigation commenced. For my part I handed the stone and a full report of my findings to the Native Commissioner and much later heard over the grapevine that the culprit was another messenger who was courting the same woman as the victim.

The French axiom – *cherchez la femme* (look for the woman) – proved once again to be as appropriate in Fort Rixon as it was in Paris.

CHAPTER TWENTY-SEVEN
Sleuth-Hounds

I cleared up all my outstanding cases at Fort Rixon and reported to the District Camp in Bulawayo to join a number of fellow district policemen all anxious to emulate the deductive virtuosity exhibited by Sherlock Holmes.

Luxurious – even comfortable – Baker Street apartments were not to be our lot. In fact, living conditions at the camp were barely tolerable. And district policemen, while being quite prepared to endure Spartan conditions – roughing it – whilst on patrol, were singularly impatient regarding their accommodation now that they had joined, albeit on probation, the "modern and sophisticated" branch of the Force.

One would-be detective found a bug in his room and complained bitterly to the Senior NCO in charge of the camp. The latter, perhaps a trifle impatient at the influx of "bright boys" and their attitude, promptly called in a firm of fumigators in answer to the complaint. The result was that the embryo plainclothes constable returned from duty to find his room with all its contents sealed to the ceiling. A large "Danger" notice, forbidding entry, was tacked to the door. The victim had to dash to the chemist for toothbrush, soap, towel, facecloth, shaving gear and hairbrush and comb before contemplating his evening bath. He slept – in a vacant, unfumigated bed – in borrowed pyjamas.

The rooms were two-bed affairs and while the CID aspirants were relatively permanent in their lodgings, the Bulawayo District Camp was of course the temporary home for the "real" district policemen with official business in town. It was not unusual, therefore, to return to one's room, tired and weary after a night duty, to find at best a new room-mate who had turned the place upside-down in one's absence or, at worst, one's bed occupied by a visitor from the sticks.

It was not long before we realised that as long as we were probationers we were expected to tolerate these uncomfortable quarters. Indeed, we were in an uncomfortable position in the broadest sense, having relinquished the status of "useful" policemen by volunteering to become plainclothes constables who ostensibly were at liberty to come and go as they pleased. There were no morning stable parades for us, no spit and polish for Saturday morning inspections and no arms drill or musketry parades.

Personally I found the abrupt change of atmosphere – if not of environment – very hard to take. A bicycle replaced the accustomed horse but we did receive a cycle allowance; instead of extra-mural parades (and we had to put in a full day of "investigations" besides our schoolwork), we were shepherded into lecture rooms to learn the intricacies of classifying fingerprints. Cycling in fine weather was not unpleasant, but when the weather turned wet and cold, splashing through the suburban compounds became most unpleasant – and most undignified.

These trials we were expected to endure for six months before shedding the lowly title of PCC to become full-blown detectives. I never reached such distinction, chiefly because of the treatment received in the camp which had once been the most hospitable place for a visiting district policeman. But before requesting a return to the mounted branch, I did get a taste of one or two interesting cases.

The first case was a sour one and one which underlined the gap between the CID and uniformed branch. There had been a large scale theft of building equipment from a Bulawayo hardware concern. From "information received", I discovered that the stolen property had been cached no more than a stone's throw from Nyamandhlovu Police Camp. Rather proud of my "source", the sergeant at Nyamandhlovu was somewhat taken aback when I turned up at the camp unexpectedly, took him and a couple of labourers to the nearby cattle kraal and quickly retrieved a large quantity of nails, screws, bolts, hammers, screwdrivers and the like. Among the accused was an old employee of the hardware company who from time to time had quite legitimately purchased tools and other items from his employers. It was decided not to prosecute the employee – discharge was sufficient punishment and also avoided the complication of distinguishing between those items bought and stolen.

This kind of horse-trading quite understandably didn't go down well with the policemen at Nyamandhlovu; nor did it ease their embarrassment at having the stolen goods buried under their noses. A little more tact and less one-upmanship – of which I was as guilty as anyone – would have strengthened relations between the two arms of the Force instead of inhibiting real co-operation.

Another case had a similarly unsatisfactory conclusion as seen from the viewpoint of ordinary district policemen accustomed to working by the book. In this case, there really was no alternative however.

It was Christmas Eve and just about everyone in Bulawayo was out buying last-minute presents or merely window-shopping and enjoying the festive atmosphere. One young couple and their four-year-old son – I'll call them the "Joneses" – joined the throng and then decided to pop into a crowded bar for a thirst-quencher. Junior in his wheelchair was pushed just inside the door, out of the chilly night air, his new coat was taken off and hung on the pram handle.

A similar trio – the "Smiths" – followed an identical pattern in the course of their night on the town. But Smith Jnr had no coat. When Mr and Mrs Jones had finished their drinks – which had taken them longer than Mr and Mrs Smith, they discovered their son's coat was missing. They reported the theft to the police and I was unfortunate enough to be given this "important" investigation.

It seemed that every couple with a three- or four-year-old child had been out on the town that Christmas Eve. No one could put a name to the "Smiths", so lots of foot-slogging and ever-lasting questions seemed the order of the day – Boxing Day by this time. Everywhere I looked I saw four-year-olds being pushed around the streets or parked or playing outside their homes. It was unlikely that the stolen coat which had been accurately described would be in evidence so soon after the theft, especially during the day. All my native detective and I could do was to ask the servants at each house at which an infant was in evidence if a new coat had suddenly appeared on the scene. It was an uninspiring investigation but we kept at it for a week and finally achieved the detective's legendary "break". One servant told us a child had visited the house wearing a coat he hadn't seen before. He described the coat and the description matched that of the stolen article.

Having ascertained where the suspects lived, the next step was to get a warrant and the assistance of a woman searcher.

The wife of a town policeman volunteered and was sworn in. Together we raided the suspect premises – on New Year's Day.

We could hardly expect a warm welcome. We interrupted a party with a card game in progress and plenty of liquor being consumed. As tactfully as possible I explained my mission to the hostess who permitted us to search the premises. We looked everywhere – except in the sitting room where the party was going on – and drew a blank. There seemed no alternative but to intrude upon the revellers but first I asked the servant if he knew anything about a child's coat. He did. There was one lying on the floor behind the sofa in the sitting room.

We joined the party and there, sure enough, was the coat thrown carelessly behind the furniture. The hostess seemed genuinely surprised and could not explain how it got there. The servant was more helpful and gave the name and address of the child who, with its parents, had visited the house earlier. I had no further need of assistance from the woman searcher so I thanked her, telephoned for transport (the district motorcyclist) and made my way to the address given.

At the house in question I had no sooner slipped off the pillion with the coat in my hand than a little boy of four dropped the toys he was playing with on the veranda and came running to meet me. "That's my coat," he said joyfully. "Where did you find it?" In response to my question, he said he'd been given the coat for Christmas by his Aunt Mary. His parents, it seemed, were blameless and I still had to confront Aunt Mary with the evidence – and a possible charge of theft.

Two things brought the investigation to an unsatisfactory conclusion. Mr and Mrs Jones were so pleased at the recovery of the coat that they withdrew their complaint. And Mary Smith produced a garment similar in both colour and size – but considerably grubbier – to support her excuse that the coat had been taken by mistake.

I remained unconvinced but the case was more than enough to illustrate the painstaking, foot-slogging kind of investigation that was to be the lot of a lowly detective. This kind of work was not what I had been used to but I resisted the temptation to ask for a transfer back to my former role for a few more weeks.

CHAPTER TWENTY-EIGHT
The Great Train Robberies

The parting shot in my brief career as a detective was a resounding one, not that it gave me any great sense of satisfaction as a police investigation. As I've said, CID work was fast losing its glamour for me, quite apart from the uncomfortable living quarters we were expected to put up with during our apprenticeship in Bulawayo.

The case began, almost incidentally, when I was told to cycle to Bembesi Siding, nearly thirty miles out of town, to investigate the whereabouts of someone "wanted by the CID for questioning". Native Detective Kunatsa, my half-section, and I were hot and tired to say the least when we reached Bembesi in late afternoon. (It had been mid-morning before we had been given the assignment.) Nor were our tempers improved when we learned that the man sought had left for Bulawayo by train that morning. Before starting the long ride back, we stopped to visit the local storekeeper for a drink of water.

We got into conversation and when I told him I was from the Bulawayo CID, he retorted that I was just the chap he was looking for.

"Come and have a look at this," he invited.

I followed him into his reserve storeroom where several large bales of clothing reposed. Although they had only just been delivered – the dust of the railways bus could still be seen – by no stretch of the imagination could the consignment have been received complete and in good order. Two bales had been ripped open and a fair proportion of the contents was missing. The storekeeper, visibly upset, could offer no explanation for the damaged and missing goods. Noting down the contents of the damaged bales, which contained jackets and trousers respectively, I asked how many garments each package should contain.

"There's supposed to be a gross in each," grumbled the tradesman. "But you don't need to count them to see that about a quarter of the contents are missing."

Kunatsa and I, with the storekeeper's help, did count them and proved the latter's suspicions.

"How often has this happened?" I asked.

"Just about every consignment of goods I receive has been tampered with. Someone is making a fortune pilfering from the railways."

He went on to explain that while his losses were covered by insurance, the time and inconvenience spent making one claim after another was infuriating. I promised to find out if anything was being done in Bulawayo about the thefts and Kunatsa and I set out on the long cycle ride home.

The next morning I put in a written report to my immediate superior and I was called in later as a result.

"Look here, Palmer," he said, somewhat testily. "We can well do without more complaints of railways pilfering. Apart from being hard to prove, we just haven't the men to assign to such cases. If you go up to Mr Ramsey's office, you'll find that there have been something like 150 similar cases reported already this month."

I was astounded. "Has nothing been done about any of them?" I asked, quite forgetting my lowly position of plain-clothes constable.

"Well," replied my boss – to his credit almost shamedly, "there is this one case of Europeans stealing petrol at the siding but it is still under investigation."

I continued to argue: "Petrol is one thing, but what about pilfered goods which are easily identifiable, more easily traced?"

The only answer I got was a shrugging of shoulders and the return of the report which I'd made.

The policeman in me was far from satisfied. There was little to be gained by seeing Mr Ramsey in the Charge Office and confirming just how many thefts of goods under consignment had been reported. Instead, I went down to the railways warehouse the next morning, introduced myself to the superintendent on duty, told him what I had witnessed at Bembesi and asked if he could shed any light on the matter. By way of reply, the superintendent bent down beside his desk and produced an empty five-pound tin which had recently contained Macintosh's "Toffee de Luxe".

"What's this?" I asked, somewhat mystified.

"It was handed to me by one of your native policemen as he went off duty this morning. Now you have another crime to add to your long list."

"Where was the tin found?"

"I don't know – but it is obvious that it was stolen from a railways consignment of sweets."

"And it was found quite empty?"

"Yes."

The conversation wasn't very helpful but perhaps the thief with a sweet tooth hadn't entirely cleared his tracks behind him. I asked the superintendent's permission to look around. He readily agreed but doubted if I would find anything.

The warehouse was a solid structure of wood and iron raised on redwood pillars designed to discourage termites. Around the shed was a solid security fence – diamond-mesh, vermin-proof netting topped with thief-proof(?) barbed wire. At one point a litter of paper had been blown against the fence. I strolled over and picked up one of the pieces of paper.

The toffee's in my tummy, the tin is in the burn.

Bang went Sixpence – but it was worth it!

The printed message beside the picture of the Scots laddie in kilt and sporran told me I was at – or near – the scene of the crime. Using my common sense, rather than any of the deductive techniques I had so uncomfortably absorbed in the preceding weeks, I retraced the trail of the sweet papers to one of the redwood pillars. This was where the felon had consumed five pounds of toffee. There was more.

Apart from being an "inside job", the clear impression of the heels of hob-nail boots indicated that the thief was one of our own native policemen – only they wore this particular kind of boot.

I was very satisfied with the results of my initial investigations but I would have to tread warily – more warily than my fellow police officer of the sweet tooth. I decided to keep quiet about what I had discovered and to keep a close watch on the warehouse in the meantime, especially at night. Discreet enquiries revealed that the African personnel at Raylton Police Station were unusually clannish. In fact, almost to a man they had been recruited in Barotseland. In such circumstances, getting any one individual to spill the beans was most unlikely. I needed more than suspicion and circumstantial evidence to prove my case.

I had learned to trust Kunatsa implicitly and took him with me that first night to the warehouse hoping to catch a pilferer redhanded. But to reach the goods shed one had to pass beneath a causeway and no sooner had we done so than a human whistle pierced the still night. An answering whistle came from the direction of the warehouse. Kunatsa insisted it was a nightjar's call but he was talking to a district policeman. Not unexpectedly we arrived at the goods shed to find all in order – the guards from Raylton Police Station alert and putting on a good show of "protective custody".

The following night I took the precaution of extinguishing my cycle light before nearing the causeway –and told Kunatsa to do likewise. The night birds were silent this time. At the warehouse the discipline of the previous night was somewhat lacking but although we watched carefully for several hours, I eventually had to give up the surveillance without uncovering positive evidence.

I had other assignments and found it impossible to spend more time on the pilferers. However, I asked Kunatsa to devote as much of his spare time as possible among the constables at Raylton, keeping his eyes open for incriminating evidence of any kind. In particular I told him to be on the look-out for the jackets and trousers which had brought us into the case.

Nothing happened for a couple of weeks. Then, one Saturday midday, Kunatsa rushed excitedly into my office to report that he had seen two Raylton policemen wearing the "Bembesi uniform" – one had on a jacket and the other a pair of trousers both identical to the items we had laboriously counted under the storekeeper's direction.

It was all I needed. Hastily I typed an application for a search warrant which would authorise me to examine the kit and personal effects of the two constables. At 12.45 p.m. I placed the request in front of my superior who, as a Justice of the Peace, could issue the warrant. But it was a few minutes before locking up for the weekend. Getting the warrant was no matter of course and still another brush with authority loomed.

My suspicions regarding the nefarious activities of policemen stationed at Raylton had been confirmed by Native Detective Kunatsa who had seen two of the policemen wearing items of pilfered clothing. Getting a search warrant authorising me to pull the Raylton Police Camp apart would have been difficult at any time. The fact that it was minutes before Saturday's one o'clock closing-up time when I put the warrant application before my superior for his signature helped not at all.

He stared aghast at the document, then refused to consider it.
"You had better see the Old Man," he advised curtly, referring to the CID Chief Superintendent. "See what he has to say about all this."

I rushed upstairs to the sanctum, knocked on the door and entered after an intimidating "Come in". Standing to attention, I handed over the application which – to give him credit – he read attentively. Then he transferred an equally attentive gaze to me.

"Have you reported this matter to Inspector Perry?"

"Yes, sir."

"What was his response?"

"He told me to come and see you, sir."

"Hmm ... you realise, don't you, Palmer, that you are one of my most junior men and here you are making a very serious charge against two fellow members of the Force?"

I told him I was aware of the implications but that I wouldn't have requested the search warrant unless I was sure of my facts. Kunatsa, who had been waiting for me, was called in and thoroughly questioned. Our combined stories must have convinced the OC because he retrieved his pen (already in its holder for the weekend) and signed the warrant with a flourish. I thanked him and returned to Inspector Perry.

"Did you get the warrant?"

"Yes, here's the old man's signature. Now, have I got your permission to grab as many of the native constables as possible to help in the search?" It was three minutes to one o'clock.

"I suppose so – take the lot. But you're not going now, are you?"

"Yes, sir. I must strike while the iron's hot."

Between Kunatsa and I we were just in time to halt most of the constables in their tracks before they made off for the weekend on their cycles. I even recalled a few of them as they were riding through the gate. My task force numbered twenty-four and I carefully briefed them in their own language on our assignment.

Raylton Police Station was relatively securely fenced in with about a dozen strands of barbed wire. Kunatsa and I would carry out the actual search while the remainder of my men surrounded the station to ensure that nothing was passed through the fence. My small army of policemen climbed on their cycles and joined the heavy lunch-time traffic bound for Raylton.

Our invasion could hardly have gone unnoticed but when I

enquired for the sergeant-major in charge, I was told he had gone to his quarters. Meanwhile, much movement in the native lines indicated there was no time to be lost. I almost ran to the sergeant-major's quarters and pounded on the door.

"Who the hell's that?"

"This is PCC Palmer," I replied. "May I see you in your office, immediately please, sergeant-major?"

"All right," was the reluctant response. "I'm coming."

As we walked back to his office, there was no disguising the sergeant-major's mood.

"You young blokes are always looking for promotion – don't you ever do any real police work?" He used a stronger term than "blokes" and he had yet to hear of my mission.

Once inside his office, his bootlaces undone and rubbing his eyes after the rude awakening, he asked me what I wanted. A second rude awakening, when I explained my suspicions and produced the search warrant, brought him fully to his senses. He did however have the grace to realise the gravity of the situation, although he mentioned that he had conducted a kit inspection that morning and had found nothing untoward. This in itself was almost an admission that the guard duties of his constables laid them open to temptation.

He bellowed for the two suspects identified earlier that day by Kunatsa and named in the search warrant. We then escorted them to their quarters. The barrack-room still showed evidence of the kit inspection, each bed having at its foot a substantial wooden box some five feet long, three feet wide and two feet high. Each box was the only receptacle for each constable's private belongings. The first accused – he was wearing neither pilfered jacket or trousers – was asked to identify his box. He did so and was then told to open it. Stammering – with guilt all over his face as far as I was concerned – he replied that he did not have the key. Then came a dramatic turn. One of the accused's many colleagues, peering fearfully through the door, shouted that the indicated box was his – the suspect's belongings were in a box at the other end of the room.

It was high time for stern measures and, once again, my knowledge of the Silozwe tongue came in useful.

"What's all this?" I shouted angrily in the vernacular. "Can't Raylton policemen tell the truth when they are questioned? Where are the keys? Hand them over at once!"

"The keys are in my greatcoat in the office," responded the

suspect resignedly.

Kunatsa was sent with the man to fetch the coat and as soon as he returned he showed me what he had found in the pockets. Not only were the keys there but, more interestingly, a dangerous-looking, home-made knife manufactured – quite laboriously, I imagine – from a motor car spring and sharpened almost to razor keenness. It was an ideal tool for prising lids off boxes or slashing the coverings of baled goods. In the meantime there was the box to be examined. Laid neatly on top of the contents was a new travelling rug. Underneath was a pile of clothing in the same virgin state – quite obviously the proceeds of a protracted exercise in pilfering. We passed on to the box of the second accused – and a second brand-new travelling rug. This time it was difficult to raise the hinged lid and the reason became quickly apparent – and instructive. Wedged in at the back of the box was a substantial paper-wrapped package addressed to someone at Mission Siding, Northern Rhodesia. I opened the parcel to reveal a full bolt – all of forty yards – of dress material.

What we had suspected of being a series of fairly minor pilfering cases with, to our shame, policemen as the guilty parties, now took on a new dimension. This was theft on a grand scale and the sergeant-major was in full agreement when I suggested that we no longer confine our enquiries to the two named suspects. Virtually the whole of the Raylton constabulary were lined up and each man's possessions searched in turn. The sergeant-major was hard put to keep up with the inventory of suspected stolen goods listed against each of his constables. They had all the potential of being the best-dressed policemen in Bulawayo!

I called in my squad of native detectives and we began the process of formal arrest. Once accused and exhibits had been secured, the sergeant-major and I returned to his office where – as a matter of interest – he compared his list of stolen goods against those reported by the railways as having been lost or stolen. The equation was quite staggering.

I turned to leave, the sergeant-major's earlier animosity somewhat quelled by what we'd found. As fairly respectable policemen, each of us was appalled at the dishonesty we had uncovered. We shared a measure of satisfaction at putting an end to the crime wave and were now on much improved terms. As I reached the door, the sergeant-major looked up from his stolen property list.

"Hey, Palmer – you didn't happen to find a pair of cycle pedals among the haul, did you? They were reported stolen from a consignment routed to Alick Stuart and Company."

I was surprised he should bring up such a relatively unimportant item. Also I was tired – it was nearly six o'clock and it had been a busy afternoon. I turned in the doorway, happening to notice a cycle leaning against the outside wall of the Charge Office as I did so.

"Whose cycle is this?" I asked.

"It belongs to one of the blokes we arrested. My own bike is being repaired and I borrowed his this morning."

"Sergeant-major," I said with a grin, "the stolen pedals are on the cycle you've being using!"

It was a guess but I could see the pedals were brand new – they stood out on the battered bike like a sore thumb.

"Well, I'll be damned!" was the response.

"Of course, I'll have to take possession of the cycle as an exhibit."

"But how the hell am I going to get around? I have to be at the town station tomorrow."

"Don't worry, sergeant-major," I responded cheekily. "There are plenty of taxis around or, failing that, what's wrong with your flat feet?"

If looks could kill, he would have had a sudden death to add to his troubles.

Wearily, I climbed on my own cycle, grabbed the handlebars of the exhibit and set off after the procession of accused policemen and their detective constable escort. I gave the exhibit cycle to one of the detectives to push and pedalled slowly in the wake of the parade, trying to imagine what sort of reception we would receive when we reached Bulawayo Central. I had cause to worry. The Senior Warrant Officer, Detective Inspector Carpenter, was standing on the steps of the building.

"Ye gods, Palmer, what have you got there – the whole of Raylton Police Station?"

I told him briefly of the afternoon's discovery and immediately he realised the seriousness of the situation. The Chief Superintendent and his deputy were summoned by phone and a batch of raw recruits was sent to Raylton to fill the places of the arrested policemen. I didn't envy the Raylton sergeant-major in the problems he would have in the next few days, trying to keep his station running properly with a totally inexperienced staff.

Police Headquarters and the Commissioner were advised of what had taken place and then began the tedious business of questioning the eleven accused, including two native sergeants.

My own part in the performance was far from over. When Inspector Carpenter started taking warned and cautioned statements from the accused, they began to get awkward. Suddenly they could not understand English or any of the local vernacular languages – which message they put across in quite explicit English. They would answer the charges in no other tongue than Silozwi. None of the native constables was proficient in this language and on Saturday night there was little hope of rounding up an interpreter from the Magistrate's Court staff. I spoke to one of the awkward customers in Sesutho – very similar to Silozwi – and received a reply. Eventually we extracted some sort of statement from each of the gang.

Of course they had had time to dream up excuses – that they had purchased the goods from one or other of the Indian stores in Grey or Lobengula Streets. I hoped I wouldn't have the chore of footslogging about these shops to disprove these statements.

Inspector Carpenter was fair not only to the accused. He telephoned a nearby café and ordered tea and sandwiches for which I was very grateful. Later tea and buttered scones were delivered to the office but it was three o'clock on Sunday morning before I was able to get back to camp. Imagine my annoyance on reaching camp to find that my room had been commandeered by visitors brought in for some special duty. With the aid of my cycle lamp I found Blanco sitting on my blankets and guarding my personal effects in a tent which had been hastily erected on the parade ground. Heavy rain had fallen the previous evening and my bedding was soaked. This was the last straw. I vowed there and then to resign from the CID and return to district policing. In the process of hunting for a dry spot within the tent, I came across a telegram instructing me to report to Gwanda the next day (Monday) for an inquest.

Comforted by the thought of getting away from Bulawayo sooner than expected – even for a short period – I curled up on some suitcases, pulled a coat over me and was asleep within minutes.

CHAPTER TWENTY-NINE

Goodbye to Crime

My haste to escape from Bulawayo and the furore I had caused by arresting nearly half of the Raylton Police Station contingent was – frankly – indecent. My alibi was the telegram ordering me to attend an inquest in Gwanda on the Monday morning after the eventful weekend; my personal justification was the wet Sunday night I had spent in a leaking tent after having been ejected from my room in the camp by an unexpected visitor who outranked me in the accommodation stakes.

I suppose I could have been a little more co-operative in clearing up the mass of post-arrest documentation but by the time I had obtained a rail warrant – the Gwanda train left at nine o'clock – all I had time to do was tell a CID colleague of the Gwanda summons and let officialdom rant and rave at my absence – in my absence! As it was, I was only just in time to deposit my cycle in the cloakroom at the station and buy some fruit for breakfast before boarding the train. Only later did I hear of what went on at Bulawayo Central that morning.

The Commissioner of Police had arrived with a full head of steam up. He wanted to see me but I was sitting complacently in the train to Gwanda. The Raylton offenders were paraded and were given a verbal dressing down which raised the heavens. Then followed a different kind of dressing down. The Commissioner ceremoniously – or unceremoniously – ripped the stripes from the uniforms of the ranking offenders. The he turned his wrath on the members of the CID and – if readers will forgive my lack of modesty – berated them thoroughly for being taught their job by one of their newest recruits.

Meanwhile I was giving evidence regarding the mysterious disappearance of the Bulawayo chemist whose car I had found near Beitbridge. Some time after I had returned to Fort Rixon for the short period before joining the CID, a herdsman was driving his goats out to graze one morning and noticed a white object drop from a tree. Closer examination showed it to be a human bone. Lying on the branch of a mimosa tree was a human skeleton. The police were summoned and among the remains were found a bottle of pills and a wallet identifying the missing chemist. As mentioned before, there had been a history of financial difficulty.

The lesson I learnt was that when tracking down a missing person, a frequent gaze upwards could on occasion be fruitful.

The inquest proceedings were completed in time for me to return to Bulawayo on the afternoon train. But it was only the following day that I heard at first hand of the Commissioner's explosion the previous morning. For better or worse – where I was concerned – he had returned to Salisbury. One or two of the senior CID officers complimented me on the investigation but whether, in view of my earlier unpleasant official encounters, they were merely taking a leaf from the Big Man's book, their faint praise did nothing to weaken my resolve to put an end to my short but eventful tour of duty with the CID. My application was quickly – perhaps too hastily – approved.

Happily back at Fort Rixon, I heard that Inspector Carpenter had taken the "Great Train Robberies" through to a successful conclusion, some of the culprits getting the stiff terms of imprisonment they deserved for betraying the trust placed in them as policemen. A gross (an appropriate measurement in the context of the nature of the crimes) of pilfering offences was satisfactorily closed.

Before leaving the Bulawayo affair, let me say that Native Detective Kunatsa and Inspector Carpenter deserved as much – if not more – credit than myself: the former for his powers of observation and the latter for his tenacity which included enquiries beyond our borders, proving the accuracy of the original consignments as well as recovering much of the pilfered property from Northern Rhodesia where it had been mailed to the relatives of the accused.

CHAPTER THIRTY
Spiritual Homecoming

One of the first patrols to which I was assigned at Fort Rixon involved a raid on a farmhouse near Insiza Siding to apprehend gamblers and trespassers – a much appreciated "routine" investigation after my Bulawayo adventures. In fact all it required was a single surprise nocturnal visit to the premises in question. The offenders were easily netted and were sent off at dawn the next day to Fort Rixon escorted by the native constables who also took my pack animal.

Meanwhile I had received an equally routine report to investigate the discovery of the mortal remains of an alien employee at a nearby farm who had disappeared some twelve months earlier. With the Gwanda inquest still fresh in my mind, I was less than surprised to discover that a convenient tree had claimed another suicide victim. At least this time I didn't have to go looking for the body.

I met the farmer as arranged and together we rode up the long valley to the spot some three miles from the homestead where there was a large thorn tree. An element of sick comedy greeted us. The eyeless skull gazed down the valley up which we had just ridden, held in position by a reim around the few remaining top cervical vertebrae. The rest of the spine and a jumbled mass of whitened bones were heaped below. Among the bones was an old great-coat, so rotted as to be beyond recognition. But formal identification of the deceased was of prime importance.

With my riding crop I scratched among the remains and unearthed a leather purse. Although split around the seams, the inner pockets were reasonably intact and had served their purpose in preserving the blue registration certificate which confirmed that the suicide was in fact the missing Mloswi. There was absolutely nothing to suggest other than that he had hanged himself. Much to the farmer's discomfort, I insisted on taking a photograph of the former employer immediately below the grinning skull which I proposed to submit at the inquest. His reluctance was, I imagined, based on some peculiar superstition that he might end his life in similar fashion. I was to have cause to remember his superstitious nature later that evening.

By the time we had made arrangements for the remains to be collected and buried decently, the sun was setting. It was dark by the time we got back to the homestead and the farmer asked me in for a cup of coffee. This in turn led to an invitation from his wife to stay for supper, an invitation I had no hesitation in accepting with my pack animal and its supplies by this time probably comfortably stowed back at Fort Rixon

The farmhouse was typically built of red brick, but the main room was anything but usual. It was huge, of almost baronial proportions with massive beams of Rhodesian teak supporting a roof of unusually high pitch. The hospitality was in keeping with such surroundings. A plough disc filled to the brim with glowing embers was brought into this vast room and the three of us gathered around it, deeply appreciating its warmth on a chilly night. The unusual heating arrangements certainly lent a far superior atmosphere to that provided by the conventional fireplace. As I was enjoying the warmth and a welcome cup of coffee, we were joined by a second couple. I suppose they must have been in their late sixties, the husband with long flowing hair greying at the tips. But it was his wife who caught my attention as the introductions were made. She had the most piercing pair of green eyes I think I have ever come across – they seemed to look straight through you.

The visitors were from Johannesburg and the first indication I was given of anything other than a typical evening's hospitality was the comment that this was the last chance the visitors would have of "completing the circle" before their return to South Africa. After a few minutes of polite conversation with the arrivals and my hosts, I was left to myself while arrangements were made for what I quickly realised was some sort of séance. An adjoining room was to be the venue and into it was carried an assortment of paraphernalia including a gramophone with aluminium trumpet and a violin. My presence seemed to be a bit of a complication. Because of the house's construction, anything happening in the room intended for the séance could be heard quite plainly in the main room with its plough disc of dying embers. My host, showing not the slightest sign of embarrassment – after all, it was his house – offered me a newspaper and led the way to a spare room on the opposite side of the hall to the prepared "chapel", where he invited me to make myself comfortable. Only then did he expand on the night's programme to the extent of telling me that the green-eyed lady was a famous medium, that she would be conducting the séance at which – politely – my presence was not necessary – and that it was through her that the remains of the suicidal Mlozwi had been found.

Even a district trooper, accustomed to accepting at short notice the hospitality of some most peculiar people, this was certainly the strangest prelude to supper I had ever experienced. Telling myself that it takes all sorts of people to inhabit a policeman's beat, I tried to read the newspaper by the light of the flickering candle. But it was too much of an effort. Instead I sat back and listened to the music floating from the mysterious room on the other side of the hall. It was a tune I knew well and had played on my own gramophone many times ...

"Behind the clouds, there's clouds and clouds of sunshine for you ..." My own recording back at Fort Rixon featured just a single violin – this version had two instruments playing in perfect harmony. I strained my ears, quite enraptured by the beauty of this previously unheard version. The newspaper on my lap became completely ignored.

Totally unexpected interruption of my enjoyment came with a shriek from one of the ladies – I couldn't be sure which one of them. But there was no mistaking the scolding tones of the long-haired male visitor from Johannesburg.

"Will you please behave yourself, Casper?" he shouted above the twin violins.

Quite naturally, and innocently I suppose, I wondered who on earth Casper could be. I had seen no one other than my host and hostess and the two South African visitors, none of whom had been introduced as "Casper". But whoever he was, he was misbehaving to the extent of eliciting shrieks and shouts from the ladies and the rebuke of the gentleman from Johannesburg. Never in my twenty-five years had I heard anything quite like it and the experience made me nervous in the extreme. I rose and examined more closely the spare room in which I had been closeted. The fact that the door had been locked from the outside – unbeknown to me – did nothing to allay my discomfort. The window was partially blocked by a dressing-table but by craning my neck I could see that it was at least a six-foot drop from the window to the ground – not that I was immediately contemplating the less-than-easy way out! A door opposite the window opened readily at my touch to reveal no more than built-in cupboards. Thankfully no skeleton dropped to my feet as I opened this door and there was no line of grinning skulls mocking me from the shelves. A nervous look beneath the bed revealed no more than a thin layer of dust. Finally I satisfied myself that I was utterly alone in the room with only the flickering candlelight for company; that I was being rather juvenile in my fears and that the hot afternoon's discovery of the skull suspended in the thorn tree had set my imagination racing.

"Casper! Casper! Will you stop your nonsense!"

The loud and angry exhortation, echoing off the high-pitched roof, did absolutely nothing to calm my already nervous disposition. The volume and the agitation of the almost desperate scolding quite overwhelmed any warning of peculiar goings-on revealed earlier. It came just as I was winning the battle for self-assurance in the locked room. Returning to earth after the fright – I felt I'd jumped at least a foot off the ground – I was very conscious of a bristling in the nape of my neck. Get a grip on yourself, Palmer, I chided myself.

Almost in desperation I picked up the newspaper but I was so unnerved my shaking hands made the print unreadable. After this second, louder burst of annoyance at the mysterious Casper, there was no further indication of what was happening across the hall other than muted mutterings. But to add to my discomfort, I was famished. Apart from the cup of coffee earlier, I had eaten nothing since breakfast and there was no evidence of the promised supper arriving. I glanced at my watch – it was past ten o'clock. I would have been better off scrounging what food I could and spending the night beneath my saddle blanket. The locked door, hunger and thirst made my imprisonment very real and very intimidating.

My relief can be easily imagined when I heard footsteps beyond the door and the key turning in the latch. My host appeared in the doorway.

"Come and have supper, Palmer." He announced, without the slightest explanation of the locked door and the subsequent unusual events – or of the lateness of the proffered meal. I followed him into the baronial hall and was reassured to see that the huge table had been set out during my imprisonment. I took the seat indicated, next to the gentleman with the flowing mane. The ladies, already seated, were patting their hair in a manner which presumed some earlier physical excitement. The table talk was opened by my hostess.

"Wasn't Casper terrible tonight!"

Then she sensed my bewilderment – to put it mildly – and decided that some explanation was called for.

"Please excuse us, Mr Palmer, but we have just experienced a terrible session with Casper ... But, of course, you don't know him."

I must have looked either very naïve or utterly foolish. She continued: "None of us know him, actually. You see, he was a miner in Johannesburg's earlier days and legend has it that he was attacked, robbed and killed while taking his gold dust to be sold. His body was stripped and thrown into some prickly pear bushes where it was found much later. Since then he has wandered about looking for his clothes and his gold."

I must have seemed stupid but I could think of absolutely no suitable reply. The old man beside me saved the silence.

"That's right, Mr Palmer. And for the first time tonight we saw the materialised form of the late Mrs Carlsson."

The name meant nothing to me so I must have looked more stupid than ever. This time it was the lady with the green eyes who came to my rescue.

"Yes, Mr Palmer. And we asked her if you were 'all right', the answer was yes and so you could have joined our circle after all."

Perhaps I should have expressed my appreciation at this vote of confidence. All I felt like doing was bolting from the room. The subject was changed when I was asked if I would take soup.

"Soup!" I echoed childishly. "Yes please, I'd love some soup."

The meal was excellent in spite of all that had preceded it. We finished off with fruit salad, biscuits and cheese and coffee. The visitors then made their apologies, saying they had to be on their way to South Africa at first light and that an "early" night was called for. I expressed my pleasure at making their acquaintance – "pleasure" was perhaps an inappropriate word – and then thanked my host and hostess for their hospitality. I would have to embark on my own "Sunrise Patrol" to return to Fort Rixon.

I said goodnight and retired to my room where I sat on the bed and reviewed the strange events of the evening. What on earth had my dinner companions meant by saying that I was "all right"? Did they look upon me as a potential convert to spiritualism? Had the green-eyed lady with the piercing eyes looked right through me and decided that I was a suitable candidate to join her on the astral plane? These and similar thoughts ran through my head as I removed my boots and leggings. Tired as I was, my churning brain did not allow sleep to come easily.

The house was utterly silent. Nothing moved except the curtain fanned by an intermittent breeze from the open window which all but snuffed out the candle on the table beside me. I shifted uneasily on the bed and again wished for the familiar feel of a saddle blanket. Sleep eluded me.

The knock on one of the room's doors almost sent me through the unceilinged roof.

"What is the time, please?" came a voice from somewhere – exactly where I couldn't be sure, due perhaps to the unique construction of the house. I froze, wondering if my imagination, already fired past boiling point by events earlier in the evening, was playing tricks. Then came another knock and the same unrecognisable voice.

"What is the time, please?"

Ironic confirmation that I was not dreaming was the unmistakable ticking of a clock somewhere in the room. The ghostly question was asked a third time. The source of the ticking was as eerie and mysterious as the persistent question. Arming myself with a boot, I approached the built-in cupboards, previously described and from which the noise appeared to be emanating, and flung open the door. The seemingly increasing stridency of the seconds passing did not come from the cupboards. I turned about and moved toward the door. This time there was no doubt that the ticking was louder.

"What is the time, please?" floated into the room for a fourth time and – as I was inches from the door – was accompanied by an urgent hammering which was so close and so unexpected that I almost dived back into the bed and pulled the sheets over my head. But I was Trooper Palmer, the dauntless district policeman!

Preparing to fling boot at the intruder my imagination had now thoroughly convinced me was the mysterious Casper, I gently turned the knob and jerked open the door. There – a picture of innocence – with her tresses falling softly to a brightly-hued kimono and framing those piercing green eyes – was the lady visitor from Johannesburg. In her hands she held a large, loud but very ordinary alarm clock.

With what must have appeared to be extreme rudeness, I yelled that it was twelve o'clock and slammed the door in her face in a peculiar combination of relief, explosive nervousness and my generally overwrought state.

The lady offered no response to my angry answer – having the door slammed in her face no doubt abruptly cut off any sort of expression of gratitude. The ticking of the alarm clock diminished as she returned to her own room.

Only when all was still did I go back to bed. I can only say that slamming the door released my pent-up feelings to the extent that I managed to fall asleep quite quickly, my last thoughts being why I had been singled out for the frightening nocturnal visit by this very peculiar woman.

CHAPTER THIRTY-ONE
Back to Beitbridge

My posting to Fort Rixon after my unfortunate attachment to the CID in Bulawayo was short-lived. Soon after my "spiritual home-coming" – and despite all the fuss I had caused in Bulawayo – I was promoted to the rank of corporal and transferred from Fort Rixon back to other familiar haunts, this time to Beitbridge as member-in-charge. I took over from my old boss, Sergeant "Aussie", and discovered that my old school friend, Jerry, with whom I had fairly recently shared some amusing patrols, had the unofficial title of "motorcyclist" on our small establishment. The Immigration Officer could not possibly be confused with Jerry – the former's title was – just as unofficially – that of "Flatfeet".

As mentioned in an earlier chapter, we were entitled to an extra allowance for running the postal service and also for supervising the jail. The additional pay was gratefully received but the duties, especially the latter, were no sinecure.

One of the first cases I had to investigate back at Beitbridge was another of the seemingly never-ending stock thefts from Liebig's Ranch. Four of the culprits were arrested and subsequently sentenced to cuts and terms of imprisonment. As the local jailer, it was my unpleasant duty to administer the cuts – the first and the last time I was obliged to deal out such punishment in the whole of my police career. My discomfort was certainly less than that of the victims, but it was distasteful medicine all round. But it was part of the Magistrate's sentence and had to be carried out.

On a much more pleasant note, although he proved to be a pain in the neck, was the eccentricity of a frequent visitor to the village, the Mtetengwe Storekeeper. The nuisance factor was provided in the storekeeper's apparent phobia against using the telephone to contact his numerous friends and business acquaintances. He would insist that Jerry drop his postal work in order to relay his various messages to Bulawayo and elsewhere for supplies. Quite naturally Jerry soon tired of acting as the storekeeper's intermediary and came the day when my subordinate put his foot down.

The storekeeper walked in one day and asked Jerry to put through a call for him to the Jessie Mine Garage. Jerry agreed only on the condition that the trader passed his own message. There was a heated argument but Jerry was adamant, saying that it was high time that the storekeeper, Nathanson, learned to use one of the marvels of modern science. When the call came through, Jerry handed over the receiver and mouthpiece to Nathanson and then beat a hasty retreat to my office where he announced that the storekeeper was about to go on the air for the first time. The telephone line between Beitbridge and the Jessie Mine was almost superfluous. Nathanson bellowed into the mouthpiece at a volume which almost had the police station rocking on its foundations. The message must surely have been heard on the other side of the Limpopo and I suppose we should have charged him international rates. In addition to the noise problem there was the complication of a very Jewish accent. Eventually the garage owner, Malcolm, was made to understand that Mr Nathanson was urgently in need of a particular size of Goodyear – not a "Goodrich" – tyre and tube. Long before the receiver was replaced, Jerry and I were helpless with laughter. It was hilarious that first time but thereafter Jerry and I decided that passing Mr Nathanson's messages – chore that it was – was the lesser of two evils.

There was a regular bus service each day between Fort Victoria and Messina which, of course, passed through Beitbridge. I discovered that the bus belonged to an African, known as the "Queen of Sheba", who ran a very profitable drinking establishment in Messina. Chief source of her income, apart from the bus, was the sale in Messina of malala "wine" at the extortionate price of twenty-eight shillings a bottle.

Malala "beer" was no stranger to my palate – it was a pleasant drink with a sweet taste and a sweet bloom and not unlike a crude type of Moselle. The Mavenda, the tribe located around Beitbridge and Mtetengwe, had been making the liquor for years by collecting the sap of the Malala palm, a prominent feature of the local vegetation, in small containers and when sufficient had been collected, "brewing up" the concoction in a four gallon drum. The minor aspect of hygiene caused by the fact that the large drum was invariably one which had contained cattle dip but had been thoroughly burnt out and then scoured with ash and sand, had so far caused us no problems. However, I was a little perturbed about the "export industry" which had recently arisen and put in a report to headquarters on the matter. The answer came back that the crude liquor could not be classified as "malted beer" so no action could be taken under legislation controlling the brewing and distribution of African beer. Headquarters referred the matter to the Ministry of African Affairs and some understanding soul there decided in his wisdom that the so-called malala beer was a necessary item on the menu of the locals and that it would be unreasonable to deny them what was widely regarded as part of their diet.

Perhaps I had not made myself clear in my report but what worried me was the fact that the Queen of Sheba was selling a distilled version of the "beer". It took me some weeks to get my hands on the suspect liquor – and it cost me nearly a pound into the bargain – but what I was really interested in was where the relatively innocuous beer was being distilled into an extremely potent spirit. I ordered my African police to keep their eyes skinned for the site of the illegal still.

It was my African corporal who located the scene of operations. It was only some five miles north of Beitbridge and I decided to ride out and take some photographs of the equipment being used. The "laboratory" was well hidden in a forest of malala palms, most of which were being tapped into a collection of calabashes and oxen horns. No human figures were evident but as I approached a troop of baboons scurried away. I gave chase, mainly because my corporal remarked that one of the apes gave every appearance of being drunk.

It wasn't a difficult chase and my prey fell into a small ditch just as I caught up with him. For a moment the baboon just lay there. Then, with teeth bared, he staggered to his feet and I thought he was about to attack my horse. But the effort was too much for him and he fell back, slobbering and making the most un-baboon-like noises. There was little doubt that the ape was quite intoxicated by the helpings of malala beer he had sampled before I arrived on the scene. I left him to his hangover and returned to examine the distillation equipment.

The still was the most ingenious piece of work which is difficult to describe adequately in words. To start with there was a converted four-gallon cattle-dip drum. Over this had been carefully moulded a domed lid of clay into which a piece of thin scrap pipe had been fitted. This in turn passed through a hollowed-out branch into which water could be poured in order to condense the vapour arising from the boiling malala beer. At the end of the pipe was the final touch – a palm leaf which acted as a lip to steer the condensed liquid into a rather grimy bottle.

I never discovered who was actually operating the still – my real worry was the extent of the industry and the toxicity of the "wine" which was being sold in Messina. I sent to headquarters a second report, enclosing the photographs I had taken and also a sample of the spirit, ensuring that further fermentation did not take place in the sample by adding four corrosive-sublimate tablets. Later the analyst's report was returned. The sample registered nearly eight per cent proof spirit, roughly the potency of the locally-available whisky in its neat form. The authorities in Salisbury were, I imagine, a little upset to find out that the wholesome malala "beer", a useful dietary supplement for the locals, especially in time of drought, was being doctored into a brew which had none of the innocence of even a light wine.

I presume some sort of legislation was passed to outlaw the distillation process or to classify it as a dangerous substance at a later date. My subsequent personal involvement with the manufacture of the spirit went no further than the story told to me by my brother-in-law who was among a party of young men on a hunting expedition at Nuanetsi Ranch. In the course of their safari they came across a malala plantation, complete with still, and one of their number foolishly decided to quench his thirst with the "brew". It knocked him for six and the next morning he awoke with a terrible thirst, to say nothing of a headache never to be forgotten.

But with his first cup of water he reverted immediately into his drunken state and this process continued for several days until the raw alcohol eventually worked itself painfully out of his system. The malala spirit represented a very cheap way to rid oneself of any worries. The ensuing payments were much more expensive.

In this particular case, it quite upset the hunting party's plans for the better part of a week.

CHAPTER THIRTY-TWO
Of Snakes and Sealing Wax

As member-in charge Beitbridge I was privileged to share one of the most modern houses in the village with the Immigration Officer – "Flatfeet" as he was known to all but immigrants. He had journeyed from Mafeking on one occasion with a couple of snake-catchers on their way to this country to collect specimens to supply serum to the Fitzsimmons Institute in Port Elizabeth. In the course of the long rail journey, Flatfeet had gained for himself a thorough education in the science of herpetology. First, of course, you had to catch your snake and the officially recommended method was the tried and tested forked stick manoeuvre, the stick being placed immediately behind the victim's head. Step two involved the placing of thumb and forefinger behind the stick, picking up the snake and then "milking" the venom from the fangs into a suitable receptacle. My room-mate was so fascinated with the subject as the result of his "training" that one of his chief ambitions in life was to catch a snake and experiment. But the Beitbridge snake population seemed to have heard all about Flatfeet's education and gave him a wide berth.

Early one morning I was waiting to catch the railways bus for West Nicholson, the first stage of a journey to Salisbury where I was supposed to represent the Gwanda District at a national police conference called by the Commissioner. (At the time there was a great deal of discontent over the salaries policemen were receiving and the conference had been called to give delegates the opportunity of airing their views – or merely to let off steam as the cynics would have it). As I walked from the police station to the nearby store for a packet of cigarettes, I came near to treading on a fair-sized puff adder half-concealed in the track of a wagon wheel which had been made during the night. I spotted the snake just as my right foot was coming down on the reptile, with the result that my formerly staid progress from the office became something of a hop-step-jump contortion. Flatfeet witnessed my gymnastics and burst out laughing. At a safe distance – from the adder – I yelled back to him that here was his chance to catch a snake at last. This stopped his laughter and he cautiously approached the adder muttering "forked stick, forked stick" under his breath. Then he scanned the nearby bush for a suitable instrument of entrapment.

Meanwhile I continued on to the store, bought my cigarettes and then returned to the scene of the action. Flatfeet had equipped himself to his satisfaction with a mopani twig but even without the benefit of a lecture on snakes all the way from Mafeking to Bulawayo, I could see that the "forked stick" lacked the necessary degree of rigidity. The instrument was applied as per the book but my suspicions were correct and the puff adder merely wriggled through the fork. Flatfeet was despondent until I produced my penknife and hacked a fairly solid piece of dead wood from the side of the road.

"This is how it's done," I boasted.

Despite the sandy soil, the adder's head remained trapped while it curled the rest of its body up and around the stick. I told Flatfeet to use his left hand to pick up the snake but he pleased himself and used his right. However, with a broad grin of satisfaction on his face, he straightened up holding the adder between thumb and forefinger of his right hand. He had caught his very first snake.

In view of my absence from the station for at least a week, I had summoned all the African constables to my office for a parting briefing. They were waiting for me in my office and, as I tried to give them instructions for the next few days, Flatfeet succeeded in distracting them completely by sauntering into my briefing from the neighbouring office. He was still clutching the snake, of course, waiting for Jerry to turn up for work so that he could show him his prize. There was a mass exodus through the windows as the policemen sought to put the greatest possible distance between them and the puff adder in the shortest possible time.

I reached the limit of my patience. By way of excuse, I had a lot on my mind with the pending trip to Salisbury and the problems of trying to make provision for any sort of eventuality at Beitbridge while I was away.

"Flatfeet!" I yelled. "Will you and that damned snake get out of here and leave me in peace to brief my constables."

The offender and his offensive prize sheepishly left the office and the constables equally sheepishly shuffled back in. Jerry arrived with the returning constables and, more to give him the chance of getting Flatfeet and his snake off my back, I told Jerry what had happened and that the Immigration Officer was waiting to exhibit the reptile in his office. No sooner had I spoken than Flatfeet appeared in the doorway, his face as white as a sheet and with the snake noticeably absent from his left hand. The constabulary, less concerned about Flatfeet's condition than with what he was no longer holding, made their second hasty and collective departure. Before I could blast Flatfeet for another untimely interruption, he weakly complained that the snake had bitten him.

Jerry, who had yet to even see the snake, was first to respond to the news.

"Ah-ha," he said, almost rubbing his hands in sadistic satisfaction. "What is needed immediately is cauterisation."

Flatfeet's proffered finger was the obvious site of injury. Jerry rushed across the office to the shelf on which we kept the first-aid equipment and also a very versatile old hunting-knife of mine which had a nine-inch blade. The victim had meanwhile subsided onto a chair and was resignedly holding out his hand for the operation. Doctor Jerry wasted no time – I was still a little bemused by the turn of events and perhaps more than a trifle impatient at the second interruption of what I considered an important briefing. The amateur surgeon was quite merciless. He must have sliced poor Flatfeet's finger almost to the bone but, to give Jerry his due, he was equally prompt about sucking out the poison – blood dripping all over my desk in the process. With that stage of the operation completed to Jerry's satisfaction, he reached for the bottle of iodine, poured it generously over Flatfeet's finger and, incidentally, added considerably to the mess on my desk.

The emergency over, the next job was to find the snake and then to make sure it presented no further threat to the well-being of Beitbridge policemen – or immigration officers. Flatfeet was only too pleased to allow the snake to be killed, despite his earlier enthusiasm for herpetology. His leisurely education on the subject on the train from Mafeking to Bulawayo had matriculated in a very swift and unforgettable last lesson. It was a lesson I had learned a long time ago – in Africa the best kind of snake is a dead one!

The casualty department was still in full swing when the RMS truck arrived and I climbed aboard, with my briefing of the constables far from complete, for the first stage of the journey to Salisbury. After some three miles, one of the passengers in the rear of the lorry reported that we were being followed by a dog. Blanco must have seen me board the vehicle and decided that he wanted to visit Salisbury. I asked the driver to stop and, when we reached the first stop, Mtetengwe, I left my dog in the care of the storekeeper. Only later did I discover that poor old Blanco spent the next few days in solitary confinement, locked up in a garage with his porridge and milk pushed under the door as a convicted murderer might be fed.

There is no point in elaborating on the visit to Salisbury. Nothing came of the conference and as far as I was concerned it was a complete waste of time. But when I returned to Beitbridge, having collected Blanco from his prison, I was somewhat taken aback to find that not only did Flatfeet have his hand swathed in bandages but that Jerry was similarly incapacitated. It turned out to be another of the stupid pranks district policemen were liable to get up to when time hung heavily on their hands – hands being the operative word in every sense.

Jerry had been making up the mail one morning and had accidentally plunged his thumb into the hot wax with which each mailbag was sealed. The pain had sent him hopping around the room, Jerry providing for my benefit a re-enactment of his performance. Flatfeet had been there to criticise and – quite understandably I suppose with the memory of Jerry's emergency surgery fresh in his mind – had offered not the slightest morsel of sympathy. On the contrary, Flatfeet had laughed his head off at Jerry's discomfort. This in turn incensed Jerry into challenging Flatfeet to a stupid test of ability to withstand pain. With comparable stupidity, Flatfeet accepted the challenge.

My subordinate heated the sealing wax to melting point and gleefully covered the whole of the back of Flatfeet's hand with the molten wax. The victim didn't turn a hair. But when the ordeal was over and it was time to remove the wax, our immigration officer somehow managed to remove all the skin from the back of his hand. One would have thought the rivalry would have ended there. But no – at intervals over the next few days the contest was resumed. By the time I returned from Salisbury, Jerry had scored thirty "points" in the hot wax torture contest. Flatfeet had only half that number of victories but was still determined to show Jerry that he was every bit as tough as the policeman.

The rivalry ended in even more dramatic fashion. Jerry was very proud of the lioness that he had shot while stationed at Fort Tuli and one day, when things were slack, he took Flatfeet back to his quarters at the old Limpopo Police Camp to show off his trophies and photographs. While they were sitting on the veranda basking in each other's company and, no doubt, with a beer clutched in bandaged hands, a hawk settled at the top of the pole from which the old Union Jack proudly fluttered. Such desecration was too much for Jerry. He drew his revolver, loaded it and, using one of the veranda posts to steady a two-handed grip, pressed the trigger. What happened to the hawk, no one knows. But Jerry dropped the revolver like a hot brick and performed another of his "excruciating pain dances". In supporting the revolver with his left hand, he had been unaware that the tip of his left thumb was protruding over the muzzle. He was very fortunate not to have had the whole of his left thumb blown off.

Flatfeet had the last word. "There's only one thing to do," he grinned. "The wound will have to be cauterised." The next minute Jerry was "on stage" again as a result of a generous application of iodine to his injured member. To my great relief, Jerry and Flatfeet agreed that the scores were even and that it was time to call a halt to their mutual mutilation contest. But a combination such as Jerry and Flatfeet was enough to give the member-in-charge of any police station grey hairs overnight.

CHAPTER THIRTY-THREE
More Border Trouble

My second tour at Beitbridge was certainly eventful. Apart from "basic" police duties, the NCO-in-charge wore several other hats as I have mentioned. He was the Public Prosecutor and was expected to have everything necessary for successful prosecutions ready to serve up on a plate when the local magistrate came a-calling. Then there were the monthly, quarterly and annual returns which had to be sent to District Headquarters in Gwanda at the most inconvenient times. All this was in addition to trying to keep subordinates such as Jerry – and his Immigration Officer partner in many a crime, Flatfeet – out of trouble, of which more later. All round there was little spare time at a busy border station such as Beitbridge for real relaxation.

Somehow I did manage to find time to indulge in earnest correspondence with the girl I had set my heart on winning (and in which I was eventually successful). There were also the rare occasions on which I managed to escape from Beitbridge to press my suit in person at Shangani where her father was manager of the B.S.A. Company's breeding ranch. On one of these visits I met one of the Company's directors, Colonel Robins. I must have made some sort of impression on the colonel because he subsequently descended upon me in my office at Beitbridge. He was accompanied by a fellow director, none other than Northern Rhodesia's former Administrator and now Southern Rhodesian politician, Sir Drummond Chaplin.

Colonel Robins had a problem. He was being driven by an African chauffeur and the South African Police on the other side of the bridge objected to the driver taking the VIPs to Messina where they had business. Was there anything I could do, to ease the passage across the border of the two dignitaries and their driver? I went across to see the South African Immigration Officer and went to great lengths to explain the status of the two directors. Reluctantly he issued a temporary permit allowing all three to proceed to Messina for the necessary 24-hour period.

The permit was not abused and promptly on time the three returned the next day – with Sir Drummond and Colonel Robins taking the trouble to call at the office to thank me for my assistance.

Another "auspicious" occasion in much lower key was when a visitor from Johannesburg, bound for Salisbury, paused on his journey in his 1914 Rolls Royce. The vehicle naturally attracted attention but what was most amusing was the interest aroused in certain others. The Rolls arrived at almost the same time as a very ramshackle vehicle being driven by two Jewish merchants. They climbed out of their wreck and tiptoed reverently around the Rolls to stand before the high altar of its distinctive radiator. There they prayed in silence for a few minutes until one nudged the other and said: "Abe, it's a Rolls Royce – take off your hat, man!"

The episode may sound apocryphal but it was absolutely true and caused much amusement to those of us watching from the open windows of the police station.

But back to Jerry, Flatfeet and Jerry's new half-section, Nobby who had reinforced my twin troubles into what was now a terrible trio. As mentioned previously, Flatfeet shared my quarters while Jerry and Nobby lived together up in the original police quarters attached to the old police post at Beitbridge. These living arrangements led indirectly to a curious incident of history repeating itself and, once again, the victim was the unfortunate Jerry. Readers will remember the first patrol I made from Fort Rixon to show Jerry the ropes when my old school friend missed out on an evening of bridge all because of a caterpillar.

The modern quarters occupied by Flatfeet and me had a bathroom equipped with a shower, a most useful piece of plumbing on hot days – all 364 of them each year at Beitbridge! One day Jerry asked if he could use the shower, which was much more convenient to the station and infinitely preferable to the primitive bathroom back at his quarters. Naturally I told him to go ahead. Jerry undressed, threw his clothes on the cement floor, showered, dried himself and then started replacing his clothing. Suddenly there was a yell of pain and Jerry appeared on the veranda in just his pants. But down his back was a series of blisters, red and very ugly. I suspected the culprit after our earlier experience at Fort Rixon and examining Jerry's shirt, I found a wicked-looking centipede at least six or seven inches long. It was the insect's "red-hot poker" feet which had stung Jerry's back to the degree that it looked as though he had been branded. A few applications of boracic ointment helped to ease the sting but it was a few days before he was completely fit. This time the lesson got home to Jerry sufficiently for him to make a habit of hanging up his clothes.

As also mentioned, Beitbridge was real "snake country" and after the rains, particularly at night, one had to be very much on the alert looking out for snakes who in turn were looking out for frogs. This time it was a shower of rain which introduced a memorable episode ...

As usual, Jerry had been teasing Flatfeet about snakes (the earlier incident had by no means been forgotten) and had been insistent that Flatfeet was not to venture outside unless he was equipped with a strong torch. Despite Flatfeet's "herpitological education" travelling from Port Elizabeth with two authorities, and the proved shallowness of that knowledge in his encounter with the puff adder, Jerry insisted on a full length lecture – although Nobby may have been the real intended audience for Jerry's horror stories.

Eventually the lecture ended and Jerry and Nobby climbed on the police motorcycle to ride up to their quarters for the night. On arrival there, Jerry picked up a jug and, contrary to his own advice, went to the rainwater tank at the rear of the house for some drinking water. As he told the story, he was about to draw off some water when a huge snake cast its shadow against the whitewashed tank. There was a lot more substance in the snake's hissing. Jerry (the experienced snake charmer, of course) wasn't worried so much for himself but for his two dobermans. He called the latter to heel while keeping his eyes on the snake which was now clearly outlined against the tank. His shouting at the dogs must have frightened the snake which slithered off around the side of the building. Jerry's next thought was for his room-mate.

"Look out! There's a snake coming round to your room!"

Fortunately Nobby hadn't been with us long enough to doubt Jerry's cry of alarm or suspect that it was another of his jokes. Nobby wasn't going to be cornered in his room with a snake so he rushed to the gauze door, flung it open and leapt across the veranda just in time to verify the outline of a black object slithering along the outside wall. Nobby didn't stop running – according to Jerry – until he was halfway down the road leading from the quarters.

By dint of much persuasion, Jerry managed to coax Nobby back to the house. The two held a council of war and agreed that neither was going to bed until the snake had been found. Some of the constables, who were also quartered in the old camp, were rounded up and a full scale search was made of the house and the veranda. The stoep had screens of river reeds for privacy, but they were something of a hazard in terms of a snake's beady eyes. Great attention was paid to these screens but no sign of the snake was found and, after about an hour's search, it was agreed that the visitor had made good his escape.

The constables were dismissed and Nobby and Jerry rather hesitantly prepared for bed on the veranda as it was much too stuffy inside the house. As an added precaution they lowered their mosquito nets and tucked them in securely under their mattresses – just in case the snake took it into its head to share the warmth of their beds. Both of them dozed off, no doubt with thoughts of the encounter with the snake uppermost in their minds. So it was hardly surprising that Jerry should suddenly awaken with a yell of "Snake! Snake!" It was more than a bad dream and he was quite positive he felt the snake touch his arm. This came out later, of course.

The immediate result was utter bedlam as Jerry and Nobby tried to extricate themselves from the mosquito nets they had so carefully encased themselves in. The string holding up the nets was unequal to the contortions below and the next scene found two shrouded, pyjama-clad figures stumbling down the road with all of the haste but none of the dignity of an eighteenth-century heroine fleeing from Sir Jasper! I would have given a fortune to witness the sight but the only spectators were Jerry's two dogs who couldn't bear to remain in their ringside seats. They joined in, barking and snapping at the two policemen's billowing "skirts" and tripping the two fugitives when the voluminous mosquito nets failed to achieve their downfall.

It was only when Jerry and Nobby reached the bottom of the hill on which the camp was built that they stopped, more from exhaustion than anything else. As Jerry finally untangled himself, his doberman bitch showed her appreciation of the fun and games by licking his bare arm. Only then did it dawn on Jerry that this, in all probability, was the "snake" which had touched him in bed – and touched off the mad panic. He owned up to his over-vivid imagination and Nobby had the grace to join him in laughter. They collected the remnants of their torn and tattered nets and returned to the veranda.

Nobby was still very concerned about the whereabouts of the snake and conducted a thorough inspection of his bed before climbing in. On turning over his pillow, he swore to Jerry that the underside was warm and theorised that the snake had been beneath his pillow all the time. This prompted another search of the premises – with as much success as the earlier hunt.

Only by taking their beds into the middle of the parade square did the two of them get any sleep at all that night. At sunrise the hunt was resumed with all the constables enlisted for the occasion. They eventually found the snake – or a snake. It was a five-and-a-quarter foot cobra and was discovered in the reeds of the veranda no more than a few inches from where Nobby's bed had been. His theory regarding the warm pillow could have had some substance although I wonder if a cold-blooded snake could have left such a trace.

Perhaps a genuine authority on snakes could confirm.

CHAPTER THIRTY-FOUR
Change of Scenery

Shortly after my subordinates' further adventures with snakes, I slithered off on five months accumulated leave. The peace of Basutoland and the uneventful lives of my parents were a welcome change from the antics of my Beitbridge "children", Flatfeet, Jerry and the latter's new-found accomplice, Nobby. Having recovered my sanity, I spent another relaxing month at the coast before returning to Rhodesia and the stimulating if somewhat harrowing task of drawing a successful conclusion to my courtship of the young lady who was to be my wife at Shangani Ranch.

The five months were over much too quickly and I returned from leave to find that I had been appointed Member-in-Charge at Nyamandhovu, taking over from Sergeant-Major Genet. The area was occupied largely by European farms and I gathered that news of my impending arrival had not been particularly warmly received by the local residents. A namesake had served on the station previously and had made himself far from popular. The locals were under the impression that the new "Corporal Palmer" was the same character under whom they had suffered earlier.

I must confess that I was not terribly worried about correcting their misapprehension – in terms of personality at any rate. There was such a thing as a policeman becoming too popular with the locals. I was there to do a job and the private lives of the residents, their likes and dislikes, did not concern me to any great extent. However, my attitude did produce results – the results I wanted. I found that the Nyamandhlovu farmers in general were a most law-abiding bunch and not for a minute did they give me cause for regret at my new posting or complaint of any other sort. The Native Commissioner was himself a fine sportsman and actively encouraged the youngsters to join together for tennis and cricket – as a first-class batsman he was skipper of the team by acclaim and, by the same token, captained the whole district with the same aptitude for leadership.

I had hardly settled in at Nyamandhlovu when the calendar rolled round to Christmas. I was still finding my feet and my studied impartiality promised a quiet and even boring festive season. Some morsel of Jerry's high spirits must have been my hangover from Beitbridge days because I decided to break the ice by dressing up as a clergyman and capitalising on the real spirit of Christmas in visiting as many of the residents as possible. I was hopeful of finding room at the inn and more hospitality than I anticipated eating a solitary Christmas dinner in my quarters.

Of course there were parties in progress at virtually every house in the village, with an influx of visitors and relatives swelling the company. Everyone was having a riotous time with much more accent on the festive spirit in bottled form rather than in the spiritual sense. My twisted sense of humour, my legacy from Beitbridge, was fed by the imagined prelude to my knock on each door. "Why in Heaven's name must the padre visit us on Christmas Day!"

The first of my parochial visits was to the house of the young clerk in the Native Department who had his elderly mother staying with him. He opened the door rather apprehensively with the greeting, "Do come inside, Padre, Mother is expecting you." It was just on eleven o'clock and, sure enough, tea and scones were quickly offered. I was beginning to think my ruse had backfired on me as the dear old lady bent my ear in rather one-sided, almost confessional-like conversation. Unkindly perhaps, I found myself hardly able to contain my laughter as I was made party to all sorts of holy confidences with the odd bit of scandal thrown in for good measure. I was even afraid to tuck into the tea and scones in case my secret amusement overflowed and I choked on the proffered hospitality.

My hostess must have noticed my restrained appetite to the extent of enquiring if the tea was to my liking. I turned to reply and this gave her son the opportunity of seeing my face in profile. My rather prominent nose gave the game away.

"Mother!" exclaimed the young clerk. "It's not the padre at all – it's Jack Palmer!" With that he slapped me on the back and almost succeeded in achieving what had been avoided by my dainty nibbling of scones and gentle sipping of tea – that is, making me choke. The old lady, bless her heart, saw the funny side of my masquerade and the remainder of the tea and scones were devoured in fine style.

This first visitation put me into such a good mood – and I swear it was only unadulterated tea that I drank with the Native Commissioner's clerk and his mother – that I decided to call upon the more gregarious members of my flock.

At each house the story was the same. Glasses of beer and unopened bottles were surreptitiously concealed behind chairs, tables and other items of furniture. Gramophones were turned off and all dancing and associated high jinks were replaced with polite conversation. The impulse to substitute the policemen's trained powers of observation for a clerical blind eye on such occasions was too good to miss and my poker-faced homilies on demon drink could not be maintained for more than a few minutes before I gave myself away. Not one of my parishioners took offence at my antics, illustrating my earlier remarks about what an excellent bunch of chaps they were. They were human enough to realise that the local law had to let its hair down once in a while (especially at Christmas) at the risk of being left out in the cold altogether.

The impersonation was the talk of the village for days, but Parson Palmer's intrusion was readily forgiven.

To my credit – and to the credit of the Nyamandhlovu community spirit – this was the only occasion on which I intentionally poked my prominent nose into the private lives of my neighbours.

CHAPTER THIRTY-FIVE
Murder on the Gwaai

From the pleasures of Christmas to business – and unpleasant business at that. A trader named Hayman who ran a store on the other side of the Gwaai River phoned one day to report the disappearance of an employee. The missing African was a Mlozwi from Northern Rhodesia and he had been employed as herdsman for the span of oxen which hauled the trader's merchandise from the railway station at Nyamandhlovu to the store. The man had left the store with the ox-wagon, a driver and an assistant driver on Friday and had not been seen since. Hayman was phoning a week later.

The trader seemed to be very guarded about answering my questions over the phone so I thought the best course of action would be to bring the driver and his assistant into the station for questioning. A patrol brought them back – the driver Sebangani and his assistant Sekunye. From the outset of my interrogation, Sekunye answered my questions in an unnaturally loud voice and although I told him to speak more quietly, that his shouted replies were quite unnecessary, he seemed unable to respond in more moderate tones. The inference was that he was extremely nervous of someone or about something and that his manner of speech was designed to literally broadcast any evidence he might offer. In this way he could not be accused of revealing information which he had been told – forgive the pun – to keep quiet about.

Another ominous piece of information came to light from another source. The driver, Sebangani, was widely regarded as a witchdoctor.

I had a feeling in my bones – sorry, another pun – that this was going to be a long and complicated case and one which required very careful handling. I wrote to the District Superintendent in Bulawayo, expressing the wish to be allowed to investigate the disappearance thoroughly which in turn would mean retracing the ox-wagon's journey as far as the

Gwaai where the missing man had last been seen. In the circumstances I considered it prudent that a relief NCO be sent to hold the fort at Nyamandhlovu during my absence.

My suggestion was agreed to and as soon as my relief had arrived I set out for the wagon outspan on the Gwaai River. In the dry season there was no surface water at the crossing point which meant that it was necessary to dig into the sand to water passing livestock. Because the crossing was used frequently, a drift had been built and, since the peak of the dry season was still some months away, there were pools on either side of the drift. The lower one was the result of excavations to water cattle while the upper pool served the more permanent purpose of being used to replenish a dip tank built into the bank of the river above the high-water mark. As it was winter there was less need for frequent dipping and the tank was almost empty. What water there was in the dip was covered with green slime, another indication of its lack of use.

We had of course brought Sebangani and Sekunye with us and individually each was made to point out where they had outspanned the oxen after crossing the river. We commenced our investigations from there. More questioning resulted in Sekunye telling us that they had killed a goat at the outspan and the site of the slaughter was found. I noticed that a great deal of river sand was scattered around which the assistant driver explained by saying that he had tried to cover up the ground which had become stained with the goat's blood.

This seemed suspicious to me. Had the goat been stolen, it might have made more sense, but the goat was supposed to have belonged to Sebangani. The spot was a tiny clearing in the midst of the wild dedonia scrub (*umqhathuva* in Sindebele). It was the ideal place for a shady siesta but also secluded enough for less innocent activity. I found myself visualising the two suspects creeping up on the missing man and murdering him as he lay asleep in the afternoon. But if this was in fact what happened, why had Sekunye indicated the spot so readily? And yet I could not resist taking a branch and brushing it lightly over the scattered sand. I was concerned over what was revealed. There seemed to have been a lot of blood spilled in the slaughter of a single goat. There was even a clearly defined rivulet of black congealed blood after all this time. I thought this was worth photographing although I doubted if the blackness of the course taken by the blood would provide enough contrast against the dark earth. I got over this by tearing strips of paper and placing them over the ominous trail and, with a long exposure, managed to get a photo which subsequently showed exactly what I wanted.

My next step was to question Sekunye on the allegation that the wagon driver was a witchdoctor. No, the assistant driver knew nothing of this. Had he seen Sebangani with the horns (*impondo*) traditionally used by witchdoctors to hold their various medicines? This line of questioning had an unexpected result. As well as being the local term for the small container-horns I was asking about, *impondo* was also used to mean elephant tusk. Sekunye, with some reluctance, took me to a spot in the riverbed opposite the mysterious bloodstain and admitted that there was something buried there. After much sweated labour, the constables and I uncovered a single beautiful elephant tusk which Sekunye said Sebangani had concealed there some time ago.

The discovery helped not at all in finding out what had happened to the missing herdsman even if it did indicate that the prime suspect was a little more than an innocent and naïve driver of an ox-wagon. But this I suspected anyway and what worried me even more was that if a large and valuable elephant tusk could be hidden with confidence in the sand of the riverbed, then a body could be buried with an equally remote chance of accidental discovery. Exposed to the hot sun and blown about by the wind, the soft sand would offer no superficial evidence of a grave after a very short period, as little as a few hours perhaps.

It was late by the time we had dug up the elephant tusk so I told the constables to head for a nearby farm, the owner of which had offered me its hospitality as my headquarters during the investigation when I called there on the way to the river. The two suspects were given a measure of rope in being told to remain at the drift until I returned. Perhaps they would hang themselves with their liberty! I saddled Charcoal and continued onto Hayman's Store to find out more about the missing man.

It transpired that the employee had been a singularly nonaggressive type – in fact, he was generally considered to be somewhat childish, especially after just one cup of beer. Hayman gave me the formal particulars and almost incidentally I learned that the head witchdoctor of the immediate area was one Sebongani who lived less than a mile from the Gwaai River crossing where I'd spent most of the afternoon.

Immediately I began to wonder whether my original

informant had not confused the "Great Sebongani" with the wagon driver. There was no way of knowing at this stage. But there was already an overtone of witchcraft surrounding the disappearance and the possibility of the Number One practitioner being involved could only hamper rather than simplify my investigations. No one would come forward with information for fear of either being cursed themselves or bringing down the witchdoctor's wrath on their families. By the same token everyone would have heard by now that the police were actively investigating the disappearance of the herdsman. I rode back to the drift, realising that sooner or later I would have to seek an audience with the notorious Sebongani.

Back on the Gwaai I came upon the driver and his assistant sitting calmly in the moonlight at the side of the road. I had bought some bread and a tin of jam at Hayman's place and handed over the food. I'd been munching biscuits on the ride from the store. I watered my horse at the pool and then let him crop the succulent grass at its edge for some ten minutes while the Africans fed themselves. When all had finished their refreshments, I tightened Charcoal's girth, mounted and set out with Sebangani and Sekunye for the camp I hoped my constables had already set up.

Although I rode slowly, the two Africans kept dropping back. I asked what was wrong. Sekunye told me that Sebangani was not well and was vomiting. I had no sort of remedy with me but promised to give him something when we reached camp. At long last we got there and I handed Sebangani a drink of epsom salts which I hoped would cure his biliousness.

The next morning I was up at dawn, having resolved to get the visit to the witchdoctor Sebongani's kraal over and done with. That was when I discovered that Sebangani had vanished during the night. No one had seen him go and there was no knowing which way he had gone. He had left his blankets behind.

We set about searching for tracks and while we found his footprints crossing the dusty road, they led off into the grass-covered veld and it was impossible to follow his line of flight further. Why had the driver taken himself off? He was not under arrest and the fact that he had left his blankets behind seemed to indicate that he might return. But where had he gone in the meantime? Sekunye could offer no assistance – Sebangani had said nothing to him about leaving the camp. The whole thing was a mystery although I was sure Sekunye could have been more helpful. I instructed that a close watch be kept on the assistant ox-wagon driver at all times.

I couldn't wait for Sebangani to return of his own accord and sending a constable to look for him, with the other policeman keeping an eye on Sekunye, meant that I needed some reinforcements. I telephoned the station and asked that the corporal be sent out to assist me in my investigations. Administrative matters dealt with, I set out with only my bull terrier Blanco for company to see if Witchdoctor Sebongani could help me with my enquiries.

There was much to reflect upon as I headed for the kraal of Sebongani, the witchdoctor who held sway over the superstitious tribesmen living in the immediate area of the Gwaai crossing at which the storekeeper's Mloswi herdsman had vanished. Was there any connection between the witchdoctor and his near namesake, Sebangani, who had himself gone missing from my camp the night before? If witchcraft was at the back of either or both disappearances, it was not going to be easy getting to the heart of the matter.

I arrived at the kraal at noon to be told that Sebongani was away visiting and was not expected back for several days. Hoping to salvage something from an otherwise wasted journey, I questioned the senior wife and said I had been told her husband was a first-class witchdoctor. Unfortunately she denied this but I persisted, asking her to produce the customary "bag of tricks" – the practitioner's paraphernalia. Again the head wife denied that there were any medicines, bones or charms of any sort in the kraal and even invited me to come in, search and see for myself. I said I would as soon as I'd had something to eat.

Having found a shady spot some distance from the kraal, I offsaddled and shared a tin of bully beef and some biscuits with Blanco, my dog. Then I rested for a few hours, wondering just how effective my strategy would be. You see, I knew that a cursory search of the kraal would almost certainly be a waste of time – especially as I wasn't quite certain what I was looking for. I'd made a careful mental note of the state of disorder within the huts and, if they'd been tidied when I returned, it would be a good indication of efforts made to conceal something. It was a devious plan but the best I could improvise.

Around four in the afternoon I returned to the huts and before entering the first of them I knew that preparations had been made for my visit. Everything was in its place to a completely unnatural degree. I announced that I had no intention of leaving until the bag of medicines had been produced. I gave them until sunset to come up with the goods under pain of an unspecified threat of the consequences. At sunset I called again but there was no more evidence of cooperation.

There was a full moon that night and after watering my horse at a small pool, I saddled up and with Blanco in tow, made yet another visit to the kraal just as the moon rose bright and clear on the horizon. This time there was quite a reception committee waiting, but no bag of medicines. From a dominating position astride Charcoal, I again threatened the inhabitants of the kraal, telling them that I would continue to worry them until the witchdoctor's tools of trade were produced. If the muti was not produced, it would be a clear indication that the inhabitants of the kraal had something to hide. Fortunately, the logic of my argument was not questioned.

"No, there is nothing to hide," they chorused.

"Then," I said, "show me where the charms are and I will go in peace."

There was a great deal of muttering among the younger women and I realised that I was making progress. But patience was the key in the circumstances.

"Very well," I announced. "I shall return when the moon is above your huts. Think well on your words."

I returned to the tree which had become my "headquarters", added wood to the small fire I had made and sat smoking my pipe until the appointed hour. When I reckoned the time had come, I rode up to the kraal and broadcast my arrival.

"I have come for an answer."

Should I be accused of theatrics, I might explain that these were all part of my plan in dealing with the unhelpful but (I assumed) very superstitious occupants of Witchdoctor Sebongani's kraal. As they gathered dutifully, I asked them if they had at last made up their minds to show me where the doctor's little black bag had been hidden. The head wife came forward.

"Yes, Majoni, we have decided to show you the place."

"Good," I replied. "Lead the way and I shall follow."

Had there been an audience, it must have looked pretty dramatic as the head wife, followed by three or four of the younger women, led the way along a narrow path under the full moon with a mounted policeman and his dog bringing up the rear. We paraded for perhaps a mile in silence and halted where there were a number of "Gusi" trees sprouting from the soft sand. It was the kind of terrain favoured by springhares, antbears and other burrowing animals – including Blanco.

I was about to dismount when I noticed that Blanco was already digging frantically. "Good dog, Blanco," I encouraged. "Fetch him out." My incentive produced an eruption of sand between his hind legs and then quite distinctly I heard his paws scratching on something more substantial than sand. To build up my reputation and ensure further co-operation in case it was needed, I took another gamble.

"You see," I announced. "My dog knew exactly what I was looking for."

A chorus of exclamations of surprise consolidated the impression I had already made.

Dismounting, I struck a match and saw that my gamble had paid off. Blanco had unearthed a military-type haversack, liberally stained by its greasy contents. It was the latter which had attracted Blanco's keen sense of smell. I took possession of the bag of tricks and rode back to the kraal with it dangling from the pommel of my saddle.

With a cloudless sky above and the brilliant moon to show me the way, there was little point in remaining any longer at the kraal. I told the senior wife that I was going back to camp to rejoin my patrol and that I wanted her husband to report to the Nyamandhlovu Police Station as soon as he returned from his travels. With that I said farewell to the witchdoctor's relatives, highly satisfied that the "white man's magic" had been up to the occasion.

I reached the farm in the small hours of the morning to be told that there was still no trace of Sebangani. Perhaps it was too much to expect him to be found so quickly. All in all, I wasn't dissatisfied with the day's work as I slipped between my blankets.

There was little to be done over the next few days except continue the search for information on the missing herdsman and continue the physical search for Sebangani. It was late at night on the second day of relative inactivity when the wagon-driver arrived in camp, calmly stating that he had come to collect his blankets. No explanation was immediately forthcoming for his absence and after making quite sure he didn't pull the same trick again, I postponed questioning until the next morning. In cold daylight I received quite a shock when Sebangani was brought to me. He was haggard and drawn and seemed to have aged to an extent hardly possible in the three days of his absence without leave. The account of his wanderings – he insisted he had done no more than stagger around with his mind only half in his body – was hardly convincing, especially as he now appeared to be completely in control of himself, mentally if not quite physically. I suggested that he show me where his wanderings had taken him, a hint he rather surprisingly took. (Had he been temporarily deranged, how could he know where he had been?) With the native corporal in attendance, we set off on the mystery tour almost immediately.

It was a fruitless exercise as I should have suspected. What made it worse was that Sebangani's condition was rapidly deteriorating. His sudden bouts of vomiting became more frequent and in a very short time I realised that I had an extremely sick man on my hands. The nearest doctor was in Bulawayo which meant returning to Nyamandhlovu and putting the patient on the train. We returned to the farm, struck camp and headed at best speed for home.

Arrangements were made for a constable to escort Sebangani to Bulawayo Hospital. I still had not the slightest evidence against him but in his condition he was incapable of making the journey alone. In the meantime I concentrated on typing out the numerous statements made, in order to bring the docket on the missing herdsman up to date.

I had almost finished this chore, reflecting that progress on the case was anything but in proportion to the time and energy thus far spent on it, when Doctor Sebongani put in the required appearance. There was still nothing to link him and the suspected murder so I confined my enquiries to telling him that I had found his bag of medicines in the bush and that I was waiting my superior's permission to take them to Salisbury for analysis. He raised no objection to this course of action, although I noticed that the intention considerably increased his state of nervousness. Official permission was granted for my trip to Salisbury and the witchdoctor was allowed to return to his kraal. Sekunye, the wagon-driver's assistant, was kept in camp for the time being. Procedures governing the delivery of important forensic exhibits were stringent even in those far-off days – the investigating officer was not supposed to let the evidence stray out of his sight until they had been personally handed over to the analyst. Somewhat reluctantly I packed the witchdoctor's haversack into a large suitcase, added a change of clothing for myself, my pyjamas and toilet kit, and prepared for the long journey to Salisbury.

The trip did not get off to a good start. The passenger train between Victoria Falls and Bulawayo passed through Nyamandhlovu at the unearthly hour of three o'clock in the morning and the police station was some distance from the railway line. Flaunting the "exhibit delivery rules" to some extent, I told my servant to set off at 2.30 a.m. for the railway station with my suitcase. What happened to him I don't know, but the result was that I found myself on the train for Bulawayo with my suitcase standing next to the track at Nyamandhlovu.

I detrained at the next stop, Morgan's Spur, where lived a farmer renowned throughout the district for his dedication to his diaries. He'd kept a detailed daily record of events since the Pioneer days. His was the only convenient habitation at Morgan's Spur and I had the humiliation of arriving at his house in the small hours with no more luggage than a coat hanger which I had grabbed from my room as I rushed to meet the train. Into the diary went the cryptic entry: "Policeman arrives with coat hanger in hand!"

Although very annoyed with myself, I shared his amusement and a cup of hot coffee and then caught the next train back to Nyamandhlovu. I retrieved my suitcase with the exhibit and, twenty-four hours "overdue", I was on my way to Bulawayo and then on to Salisbury.

The few days in the capital were uneventful apart from an incidental interview with the Commissioner and an interesting analysis of the contents of the witchdoctor's bag. One of the horns was found to contain human protein and among the bones was one that was definitely human. Despite being sidetracked by the investigation into the activities of the witchdoctor Sebongani, my enquiries into the disappearance of Hayman's herdsman were still underway, not that the latter had progressed to any extent. My prime suspect in what I felt was a case of murder, Sebangani, was still in the Bulawayo Hospital.

His henchman, Sekunye, was being kept in the police camp under observation with periodic interviews being staged in hopes that he would change or add to his unhelpful version of the disappearance. There was still no real evidence linking Sebangani or Sekunye with the unknown fate of the Mlozwi herdsman.

The fruits of my visit to Salisbury – the analysis of the witchdoctor's medicines – was sufficient evidence to warrant a preliminary examination into the activities of Doctor Sebongani. As soon as I had returned to Nyamandhlovu, the hearing commenced before the local magistrate, who was also the Native Commissioner. The latter was most anxious to hear Sebongani's explanation of the human contents of his charms and potions.

All seemed to go well for the accused at the start. He was not required to plead to the charge under the Witchcraft Suppression Act and he seemed quite at ease and full of confidence as the supporting evidence was led. Until I produced the analyst's report, that is. Then he started shaking from head to foot and great beads of perspiration stood out on his forehead. After I'd read and entered the report as evidence, Sebongani was asked if he wished to question me. He looked at me with baleful eyes and declined. The magistrate then posed the all-important question.

"Will you explain to the Court how these human remains and human bones came to be in your bag of medicines."

Sebongani faltered for only a moment before answering. "I admit that there is human meat and human bones among my medicines. These came from my infant daughter who died naturally some time ago."

Subsequent investigations in this direction offered some support for his story. His daughter had died some time previously, confirmed several witnesses, but none of them was prepared to admit that they had seen Sebongani mutilating the body. That would have been a foolhardy accusation to make about a powerful witchdoctor. With no stronger evidence against the accused having come to light, the court was forced to release him. I switched my energies back to investigating the disappearance of Hayman's herdsman.

A dramatic turn came when one the jail warders reported to me that he had overheard the prisoners talking one night in the cells. One of them had mentioned that he had heard that others had seen the body of the missing Mlozwi being dried out before a huge fire at a witchdoctor's kraal in the native reserve. The master of ceremonies at this sickening ritual was not Sebongani but a fellow practitioner who lived in a different direction.

I thought that the allegations were a bit far-fetched and hardly worth following up. But we had found no trace of the body of the herdsman and a corpse was a fairly important piece of evidence in our murder enquiries. I talked the matter over with the native corporal and together we decided to pay a quick visit to the alleged scene.

For this trip we decided to use bicycles – quicker than going by horse and giving us a better chance of surprising the suspect before word reached him of our approach. The tactic worked and we arrived suitably unexpectedly at the kraal where we found the witchdoctor busy trimming homemade cattle yokes. He was dressed in the traditional skin loin cloth above which a dirty green officer's tunic looked more than a little out of place. His trimming tool for the yokes was a rasp while next to a fire were pokers of different sizes used to make holes in the yokes. He was of squat build and wicked-looking features which included a wall-eye. It was apparent that the native corporal was reluctant to question the man too closely. The reason for our visit was a delicate matter and nothing would be gained by rushing things.

My companion asked the old man for a drink of water and while this was being brought I wandered around the kraal looking for anything suspicious and, in particular, any very large heap of fresh ash which might support the rumour voiced in the cells. I saw nothing to confirm the story I'd been told. Before the supposed witchdoctor returned with the water, I discussed the lack of evidence with the corporal. He agreed that we had very little to go on. The water arrived and I responded by offering the old man some tobacco. We made ourselves comfortable in the shade of a tree and eventually I brought the conversation round to the subject of our enquiries. The old man screwed up his good eye while staring at me with the other and gave a very reasonable explanation for the rumour.

"I know nothing of that story," he said, referring to the body drying ritual. "I have been busy making yokes for many days and I always place the wood next to a fire to soften the bark. I usually do this at night so that the fire also serves to keep me warm."

We thanked the old man for his hospitality and left. But rather than cycle straight back to the station we tried to learn more about the old man from the neighbouring kraals. There was a marked reluctance to discuss him or his habits which wasn't very surprising. He was obviously held in fear and trembling and his wall-eye did nothing to soften his reputation.

Our enquiries had drawn a complete blank by late afternoon and we decided to head for home over the rougher parts of the country while there was still some daylight left. We could complete the journey along the established roads in darkness if necessary but, as so often happened, once we reached the farming area one of the farmers would not hear of us continuing on to the station and insisted we accept his hospitality for the night.

We pushed on the next morning and reached camp in time for lunch. There was a message waiting for me from Bulawayo, saying that Sebangani had taken a turn for the worse. I telephoned district headquarters immediately requesting that attempts be made to record a dying declaration from the wagon-driver. Headquarters replied soon afterwards, saying that it was too late and Sebangani was dead.

Like all bad news, the report of the wagon-driver's death spread rapidly. That evening I was told that Sekunye wished to speak with me. He was a very different man – obviously a great worry had been taken off his mind. Having confirmed that Sebangani was dead, he told me what had happened that night when I had left the two of them at the Gwaai crossing while I'd gone to Hayman's place.

"He was a very worried man, that night," related Sekunye. "When you did not return by sunset, he came to me and said, "We are finished now." I asked him what he meant and he only replied 'Why is the majoni taking so long to return from Hayman's Store?' Then he walked down to the dip tank and I saw him pick up a tin used for mixing the dip. When he came back he told me that he had poisoned himself by drinking dip.

"Why didn't you tell me this before, Sekunye?" I demanded.

"Because, N'kosi, I was afraid that the witchcraft which made Sebangani poison himself would treat me in the same way."

For the third time that day I spoke to district headquarters, requesting that a post mortem be held to confirm that Sebangani had died from arsenic poisoning. I recalled being present at a similar autopsy at Filabusi, the body being that of a woman who had been buried for over a month and the investigation taking place at the graveside. Old Doc Wallace had advised me to get my pipe going well – as his already was –

and together we raised a veritable smokescreen. I remembered how Doc Wallace had taken samples of the woman's liver, explaining that arsenic poisoning actually preserved this organ.

The post mortem examination on Sebangani confirmed Sekunye's story but nothing would induce the latter to shed further light on what had happened to the third member of the wagon team, the Mlozwi herder, at the Gwaai crossing. It went into the records as just another unsolved missing person investigation.

The murder on the Gwaai, for such I was convinced it really was, was not the most satisfactory chapter on which to close my police career. After handing over to an old friend, Sergeant Aussie, I resigned from the B.S.A. Police and went into commerce. Fifteen years later I was to meet Aussie again ... when I was to take up policing in a very temporary capacity once more.

CHAPTER THIRTY-SIX
Last Act – Hamba Palma

Handing over to Sergeant Aussie at Nyamandhlovu, prior to leaving the B.S.A. Police and stepping out into the big wide world of commerce, was accompanied by some very mixed feelings. But the die was cast and there was no turning back. However, I had the distinct impression that I was turning my back on the warm companionship, the shared excitement as well as the shared boredom, and the country-wide team spirit which one enjoyed as a policeman.

Having taken my discharge, I undertook commercial and bookkeeping courses at the Bulawayo Technical College. I even passed a few examinations. I started in commerce proper as an employee of the old Texas Oil Company. On the advice of a former school friend, I later applied to the Tati Company in Francistown in answer to an advertised vacancy on the company's staff in Bechuanaland. I got the job and fifteen years later had worked my way up to the position of Resident General Manager.

Then came a big disappointment. The company's board of directors in London had a "friend", I was asked to tender my resignation and the "friend" was duly installed in my position. I returned to Bulawayo and managed to find a position as secretary/accountant with a firm of timber merchants.

It was while I was so employed that Bulawayo experienced another dose of its periodic labour unrest. On the first day of the strike an unruly mob of some fifty or sixty stormed into the main showroom of the timber firm, infuriated by the fact that our faithful old messenger was making tea at the rear of the premises. They demanded that he join them in their "withdrawal of labour" immediately. Various members of the mob were armed with sticks, sjamboks and iron bars and others carried stones. I suppose that it was the policeman in me which made me the self-elected spokesman of management. In Sindebele I asked the mob what they wanted and, having been told, I said that I would bring the messenger to them once they had left the showroom. They were satisfied to the extent that they retreated through the heavy glass doors beside which there was a metal barrel filled with axe, pick, badza and broom handles. As I ushered the last of the mob through the doors I grabbed a pick handle and waved it above my head to punctuate my shouts of *"Hamba! Hamba!"*

My threatening pick handle removed the mob not only from the showroom but from the front of the building. In the hasty retreat and with an eye out for me and my brandished weapon, a couple of them failed to see the storm drain at the corner of the building and in a moment there was a seething, struggling mass of bodies piled to a height of several feet – arms and legs too – in the street. I couldn't resist a few parting shots with my pick handle on the prominently exposed posteriors. As the rioters picked themselves up and crawled back into the woodwork, I turned to find that three or four other members of staff had followed my example and armed themselves with the weapons so conveniently available in the doorway. Our messenger went on making tea.

However, the strike spread and an appeal was made for special constables to assist the hard-pressed policemen. This was how I came to meet Aussie again and in the fifteen years since our handshake at Nyamandhlovu he had risen to the rank of full-blown major. He greeted me warmly but there was little time for reminiscing. More urgent business awaited.

The volunteer special constables were issued with batons and put into mobile teams of eight men to a vanette. Although we had no radio, our deployment to the various trouble spots from our "base" where we were in touch with HQ by telephone, was managed quite efficiently. I was in Number Nine Squad and the frequency of our being "sent into action" was rather strange. I strongly suspected that Major Aussie was in the control room at Headquarters and, knowing that I was fluent in Sindebele and had previous police experience, was making full use of my knowledge.

One of the most serious episodes during the strike involved a mob of some three thousand which had stormed and stoned the Cold Storage Commission and was on its way to consolidate forces with other gangs of rioters in the Bulawayo townships.

The army had been called out and a line of troops with bayonets fixed had cut off the route to the township. They were not used to this kind of action and could do little more than stand at ease with their backs to the crowd in which position they could take orders from their superiors. With the mob of rioters swelling behind them, it was not an enviable situation. Things took an uglier turn when the leaders of the mob began encouraging the rioters to break through the line of soldiers.

Squad Nine arrived on the scene at this point. Apart from the baton I had been issued, I carried a light sjambok which was a relic of my Bechuanaland ranching days. As we jumped off the vanette, I cracked the sjambok in the direction of a group I assumed to be the leaders of the strikers and yelled "*Hambanene!*" ("be off with you" or "move on") As the group hesitated, I built on their uneasiness with a second crack of the whip, meanwhile advancing upon them. They turned as one man and the whole mob of thousands retreated whence they had come.

I kept on their heels with the rest of my squad in support all the way to the Bulawayo Station where the chastened rioters were ordered to disperse and return to their respective homes. So ended the strike which coined for me the nickname of "Hamba Palma".

And so ended the very last of my police adventures and *Sunrise* Patrols.

www.ingramcontent.com/pod-product-compliance
Lightning Source LLC
Chambersburg PA
CBHW071204160426
43196CB00011B/2189